Anonymus

The fat Knight

Anonymus

The fat Knight

ISBN/EAN: 9783743344556

Manufactured in Europe, USA, Canada, Australia, Japa

Cover: Foto ©ninafisch / pixelio.de

Manufactured and distributed by brebook publishing software
(www.brebook.com)

Anonymus

The fat Knight

The Fat Knight.

His Complete Career with Conquests and Collapse and Final, Marvelous Triumph.

Written in the light of Current History and State Papers on file in various Castles in Columbia.

His Aids and His Actions

....and....

The Magic Scup.

In Three Cantos.

U. S. A., A. D. 1896.

ACKNOWLEDGMENT AND EXPLANATION.

The author acknowledges, with pleasure and gratitude, benefits afforded and utilized in THE FAT KNIGHT, aids derived through reading the *Record*, of Chicago; the *Times-Herald*, of the same city; the *Mirror*, of St. Louis; the *Argonaut*, of San Francisco; *Town Topics* and the *Sun*, of New York, the benefits accruing being slightest from the journal first named, greater from the second, and so on increasing from the newspapers in the order given, the most from the last—the *Sun*—the author's daily companion, critical counselor, valued friend and never-ending delight. The authors and masterpieces this work suggests are so clearly indicated by the method that to name them would be superfluous. The credit for whatsoever merit may be found is largely due to the specified and a few other newspapers, and to the authors and books THE FAT KNIGHT must recall. The defects, like the general run of editorial Italics, "are our own."

THE AUTHOR.

Invocation.

Complacent Dullness! Profoundest king, kind, best!
Upon talc throne in sage, suspired state,
To thee we come, like thousands who have pressed
Solicitous, beseeching favor great.
But not pelf's place, ambition's modern aim,
But boundless blessing thou, king, hast to give,
Which, if withheld, we dieth, blighted, lame,
But grant'st thou free, then might immortal live.
Thou art supreme! None other canst thou touch,
Let him be Spanish, Scotch, Hun, Mexican, Dane, Dutch.

O grant begged boon! Above us raise thy hands
Like holy priest when he dost soul assoil!
Give us thy blessing; make us thy commands;
Pour on our head thy consecrating oil!
Show us true way to praise thy foremost son—
To trace his rise, fair progress, swift success;
In spirit leadeth as his course we run;
Thrill, cheer us, spur, befriend, full favor, bless!
Such, Dullness, do! E'er with us keep in touch,
As with staid Spanish, Scotch, Hun, Mexican, Dane, Dutch!

You may say what you please, or swear it, or sing,
But plainly the pull, not the play, is the thing.

Birth, Parts, Person.

As babe: brave boy: wise youth at work
In store industrious as clerk;
His advent, studies, person, nose;
Scup; all that future greatness shows;
Precise set forth, as ought to be
In this, Fat Knight's, whole history.

GENESIS.

CANTO I.

IN this home of hustlers, leal land of keen knave,
Once lived rare reformer fat, gelid, glum, grave,
Steatopygous, shallow, sham, solemn, stolid,
Firm "sot in his ways," self-satisfied, solid;
His triumphal trait, chiefest characteristic,
Chaste honesty stern, mature, marked, majestic.
Of him we glad sing. With harp, tam-tam, lute, lyre,
Sear soul all aflame with Promethean fire,
We lumptum, lilt, elate. Like Milton, Rookh Moore,
Sappho, Swift, Gilder, we expect to explore
Hell, heaven, earth, fads, folly, fate, fashion,
Politics, platitudes, pie, people, passion,
In true epic, too, with conflict, gore, logic,
At length's all relating to vital Scup Magic
Inciting fierce war as savage, vile, hellish
As rude slaughter Virgil didst vivid embellish.
Long have we delayed. In procrastination
We galled like gallant in vain fascination
Since so much is uncertain. F'r instance, if Wilde
Were perjured to prison, or fierce, foul defiled;
If Davis when caught had, as some still assert,
Wooden pail on left arm—wore his faithful wife's skirt,
Or storm-cloak, as Stedman, thro' trenchant "Dan Quin,"
Didst graphic detail; if high-kicking is sin;
If Dave Tod with Stanton connived to let loose
John Morgan when John was of damned little use;
If God spake to Moses—they walked chums side by side—
Or Moses to Egypt monumentally lied;
Had Jesuits smooth, as their foes swear, or bray,
Studied parts in fell plot of Booth's bloody play;
Were John Brown half crazy, or'd Hannibal's head
For tactics, war, conquest, as Vallandigham said;
If Beecher so florid, fit, fervid, e'er did
Forget God one moment—nefandous nest-hid;
Were Grant—hearken, Halstead!—all honor Grant's clay!
So disgracefully drunken near front in flush fray;
If Stokes murdered Fisk, or bold, big Erie Jim
Were gunning for Edward with intent to do him;
If Keppler had reason to cari'ture Blaine,
Tattooing him fatal, through Gillam, with stain;

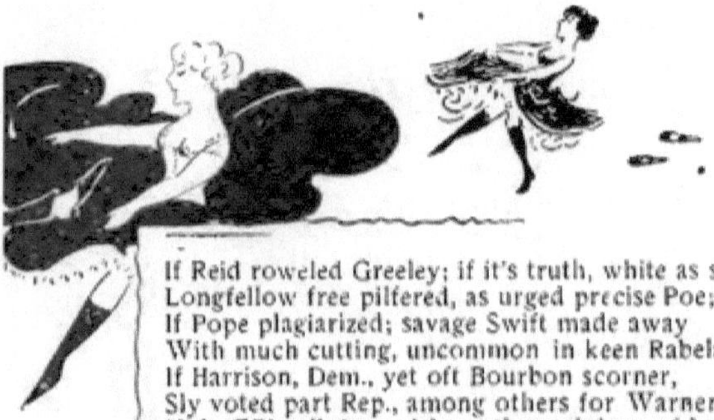

If Reid roweled Greeley; if it's truth, white as snow,
Longfellow free pilfered, as urged precise Poe;
If Pope plagiarized; savage Swift made away
With much cutting, uncommon in keen Rabelais;
If Harrison, Dem., yet oft Bourbon scorner,
Sly voted part Rep., among others for Warner;
If chuff Bissell stepped down through love of lex—law—
Or because of request; what Parkhurst once saw;
If Gilder, pure poet, so splendid in verse,
E'er versatile acted as Grover's wet nurse;
If Cleveland in anger, like drab drunk in ditch,
Spat out foulest term perfect rhyming with pitch;
If Cæsar heard thunder, as bold didst decide,
According to Plutarch; how Deist Paine died;
How Hume, Voltaire, Hobbes; if Bob'll recant
When dread rider rings, or jeer, joke, thunder, rant;
If Toxophilite Tell spurned hard tyrant so
After piercing Swiss apple; how much does Hoke know;
If Tilden, as Dana'll contend all his days,
Were defeated to deify Rutherford Hayes;
But naught is more certain in God's searching sight
Than birth of fine babe who became famous Fat Knight.
It is not recorded, as of Cherbury's lord,
Night time to clock minute fated coming occurred,
But there's extant tradition when baby appeared,
Pert, little, red fellow bed attendants all scared,
For after safe advent, remarkably soon,
Strange babe direct pointed to tide-ruling moon,
Which in pale effulgence, with argent bedight,
Earth, ocean, still heaven, soft silvered with light.
Spare, queer Galen present, vain, gray-headed leech,
Pinch'd into gold snuffbox, making slow, pompous speech
"He'll be man superb, sir! That is, if he live
To take wise prescriptions approved him I'd give.
Most wonderful babe, sir! You saw with surprise
Him pointing to Luna, fulgid thief thieves despise.
That, sir, is portentous! Shows sure, so I ween,
Sharp babe when man grown shall be bright argentine
Celestial Dian, so Shakespeare didst settle,
Is glittering goddess of sound, silver metal,

In which Western state, homage paying grotesque,
Theatrical queen men may mould statuesque,
For actor, like actress, for press praise, poor fame,
Would aught do to brighten—yea, tarnish stage name.
But about ruddy babe. Far West e'er may hold
He'll always prize silver, always deeply damn gold.
Be he sheriff, shrewd lawyer, sound teacher, stiff sergeant,
Proud major, plain may'r, or what, he'll be argent,
Indicative that, though not infallible,
He'll be sonorous, safe, ductile, malleable;
Become highly polished—perhaps in ascendant
May, as blazed Villiers, be regal resplendent.
He'll like silver rivers, "silver slumber"—clear voices
In which you may see Faerie Spenser rejoices;
As fisher you'll find he'll be where fast biting
Is principally done by silver surf-whiting,
Though he'll not disdain, with hook, line, lead'n sinker,
To bob for kisutch, friar, tailor, or tinker;
Slim billfish also, glutton nothing can fatten—
Gar Tylosurus longirostris in Latin—
Along silver streams he'll likely pursue,
As mild anglers for men with Christ used to do;
Tarpum, silver-bill, trim diver red-throated,
As loon—velvet scoter—so very wide noted,
He'll probably hunt with more or less luck
When oft in loaned vessel he ventures for duck;
Hence, folks, we may argue he'll dive into cause
As Blackstone, Coke, Chitty, ripe reveled in laws.
Babe bijou'll persist. He'll plunge down to bottom,
Or press pliant agent to hunt bottom for 'im,
As kings, queens, protectors, Macaulay makes glow,
Didst oft in old England years—ages ago.
He'll naught take for granted, but to palpitant heart
Go true as stiletto, or savage's dart.
When squat-buttock width, not worth, is held high;
When groin girth is greatness—big paunches please eye;
When fat is in favor; when party regard
Less honors deep learning than human leaf lard;
When full many statesmen, so-called, dub'd profound,
Are poor in small pates, whilst vast vest around:

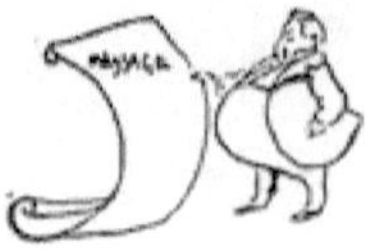

When some who succeed—are held worthy to mate
With potent renown—just depend upon weight;
When per avoirdupois, not sterling, strong sense,
Muffs measure out station, design land's defense,
Reforms, flat inaug'ral, void message exact,
Recalcitrant veto, trade, treaty or pact:
When freedom's own country elects for its chief—
When worships, not calf, but coarse, bull Eastern beef;
When revered is thick neck, though it would disgrace
Huge shoulders of Atlas, who holds world in place;
When such things appear astounding some few,
Perhaps—we can't tell—in far year '92;
When soul of tough Hick'ry above, or below,
Storms—curseth like pirate to see scrub, seedy show,
Keen babe, then man mighty, if he doth but live
To have prime prescriptions approved him I'd give,
Wilt probably league with tried troupe true as steel
To save putrid nation.
"This babe is not veal.
He's well-set, wight, sturdy. I cannot detect
From plumb head to pink heels faintest sign of defect.
But moon being full—babe taking so to it—

We may have, perhaps, some reason to rue it.
Night's eye's bizarre orb. She was Cowper's delight,
He crying white crescent's quaint crown of calm night,
Or diadem dædal. Serene she sways tide
As groom fond is fettered by amative bride.
As satellite menstr'al her orbit completes
She affects men's affairs, brains, bacon, beer, beets;
Hence, I do fear me, nimmer wan may incline
Bold babe to affect in some way saturnine.
He gloomy may grow—be gross, dull, dead, sedate;
Sluggish, sad, dismal—very heavy debate
Like pious, gowned monks in gray cloister, belt, cowl,
Or, beg your pardon, horned, acute-hearing owl.
But spoke of disc pallid. Noctivagant jade
In stolen tinsel, like vain authors arrayed,
When daintiest dressed is never too bright,
But, tarnished her togs, dun-mottled garb white,
Dim shines like wit shabby in late, loud campaign
When Van was victorious. Rival jests how inane!

Satire scowls sullen; sour sits she sans hope,
Morose mourning Butler, Swift, Steele, Byron, Pope,
Since almost is certain world's seldom had wits,
Such eagles succeeded by peewees, jays, tits.
Not that recent writers cannot provide fare
To please Attic palate, but contemn common care;
Scorn close, thoughtful study; habitually steal;
Revamp; purloin thunder; styles stupid reveal;
Mart mawkish verses; pen pestiferous prose;
Plant cockle, kale, nightshade, not lily, oak, rose."
Then Galen, like Muller, or Herder, to scan
Through cheirosophy aged, picked up pudgy man,
August, shrewd discoursing, being lymphatic learned
In all on chei subject all men hath discerned,
Having read all savants wrote long before Job,
In classical Greek, about hands, mounts, lines, lobe;
Of secrets of Albert, who had rare receipt
To prepare "Head of Glory" for thief, or caged cheat—
Who held hand of felon, hanged high for hot humors,
By touching would cure all warts, fidgets, tumors,
As told us by Hazlitt, written also by Fraser,
So make no excuse for giving lie place here.
Doddered doctor could tell by tip of blunt thumb,
Or Lucifer out-lied, all events to come.
By shaking your hand, or scanning your nail,
He'd prove if you'd prosper, get pox, bilked, or bail;
He knew from best Latin hard, brute ultimatum
When mob indicated vertere pollicem;
Why men gnaw'd, lick'd their thumbs; why nigh everywhere
Men raise hands in court—oft, too, whilst at prayer;
Why poltroon is so-called—how grew so by stages
From cowards who'd fight not in fierce, Roman ages.
He hadn't read Allen, but "Die Kunst Ciromantia"
He knew quite as well as Quixote La Mancha;
John Kidd he adored, but Humphrey, like Owen,
Not having then written, was to Galen unknown,
But of palms, joints, thumbs, fingers in whole, or each tip,
He knew quite enough twenty worlds to equip.
Knew what each hand meant. He'd elucidate
Allen's seven odd types—Mixed; Spatulate,

That's active, so often called hand necessary:
Ominous manus barbigerous—hairy—
Or Conical, Square, Large-Palmed, Philosophic;
Thin limber hand Pointed, or psoric hand psychic.
As to lines: as to mounts named for sky-studding stars—
Jupiter, Saturn, Mercury, Venus, Moon, Mars—
With great God Apollo, whose Vatican hand
Some say is so shocking, so base was it planned;
Blue line cephalic; glorious girdle of Venus;
Signs signal on thumb, but not on pent—('tween us,
Sub rosa, Latin just there we intended
Omit fearing Kansas might hold law offended,
Sunflower, Pop scapegrace being lynx-eyed for rhyme,
Or prose, counted shady, whilst commits constant crime
Ten thousand times worse. But strumpets there are
Each anxious in Paphos to reign raging star)—
He'd talk without ceasing, would write, or hot squabble
Like hosts stiff on tariff though scarce fit to cobble.
Being so well supplied in cheirosophy's store,
So full of theme's Latin, loose lingo, lies, lore,
You may well give attention to every presage
Cultured Galen delivered—here we start on this page
"This hand will be large. That is, if babe live
To have tried prescriptions approved him I'd give.
It's firm, spatulate hand. From that, friends, I reason
Babe'll nobly excel in all but in treason.
About such hard hand there's nothing magnetic,
But's resolute, active, firm, energetic.
He'll be self-reliant. He'll seek to control,
Naught but famed abundance wilt sate supreme soul!
Enough would be empty. Deep, shore-scorning sea,
Alps-covering ocean, such prodigy he
Shalt all sweep submerging! Stupendous invest!
Rule potent, grand master on apex at rest!
Him enough would distress! Enough gall—enrage!
Enough would be fatal! He'll astound every age!
Bellic Cæsar, Napoleon, hosts, fleet of men free,
This child shalt become! Earth's Omnipotent be!
Hope's ark on Ar'at! Land's buckler, shield, sword!
Columbia's savior from loins of blest Lord!

His second son earth-sent! He, pistic, like first,
Shalt, even foes saving, be mocked, reviled, curst!
Yet serenely forbear.
"Babe as man wilt deplore
Soft state Rome Augustan didst almost adore,
More favoring Draco. Babe'll not be romantic,
But banal had been had this hand been conic.
You see here large thumb—long phalanx of logic?
Grand thing to thank God for! It's characteristic
Of great men—women, too, for some shes succeed,
Although mediocre charms most of soft breed.
He'll crave creature comforts—some things that conduce
To elegant taste, like art, roasted goose,
But in such respect world's fashion he'll follow;
For finest in art quite Bœ'tian, dull, hollow;
He'll prefer what is real in each situation,
As horses, ducks, dogs, tugs, yachts—navigation.
Best method of warfare wilt frequent employ
His hope, his heart, hands, as man, chief, sturdy boy.
In administration he'll combine with rare skill
Of Hamilton Jackson's stiff, resolute will:
In all that he does—in active pursuit—
True motif you'll find at firmly-fixed root.
He'll be, I must say, very much egotistical;
Ten to one, too, he will be Episcopal.
Self-centered he'll stand. He'll not give rodent's rim
For any damned man caring not damn for him.
He'd be careful colonist, but country like best
Yielding most riches North, South, East, or West.
He'll be sensual, too, to certain extent,
As I plainly can see from way thumb is bent;
He'll not be refined, nor will he be rude;
He'll have no objection to some solitude.
He'll revere works magnific. Wild ocean, alp,
Serrated-ranged Andes, Pike's Peaks, hoary scalp
Of sky-piercing granite! Niagaran falls!
Tempestuous grandeur! Thunder's earth-quaking calls!
Cloud mountains growling! Gigantean forms!
Cyclones, tornadoes, sea-sky-lashing storms!
Lightning-rived nature! Earth's cones molten-lipped!
Ætnas convulsive! Mount Hoods fire-tipped!

He'll hug mathematics; e'en espouse, worship work—
Love physical labor, so detested by Turk.
Be avid—want wealth, cool million to him
Tiptopping, towering o'er all seraphim.
He'll yearn for substantials—all things business-like
Tho' slow empire spurring, or building farm dyke;
Be strict, stiff, tyrannic, yet legally just;
His language forcible; be true to each trust;
Firm, cold, industrious, close, persevering,
Disdaining obstruction; naught ever fearing,
But difficult tasks even often wilt court,
To sweep away obstacles as if in sport.
He'll seek to command; he will not brook restraint;
He'll give small attention to any complaint.
He'll stand tenacious; fight fell like balked bison
For all vested rights—for all things that are his'n.
He'll not be long living till he'll be commencing
Hunting, duck shooting, tautog fishing, fencing,
With everything else that satisfies life
Of men made for movement, high enterprise, strife.
In religion he'll reason. He'll seek to be certain;
He'll pull from dark future thick, Catholic curtain;
Be pious, clean, holy, so ministers say,
As some time on earth pure, immaculate Quay.
Steve'll oppose Roman faith—at least, not belong
To Christ's church impressive with incense, shrines, song,
Crosses, bulls, glamour, beads, saints, mitres, copes,
Relics, monks, convents, red cardinals, popes,
Whom point-fingered people, away in suave South,
Poetic, warm, mystic, wouldst kiss in proud mouth,
Or, knees pressing earth in mean attitude low,
As debasing as dogs, fawning lip papal toe.
No; he'll none of that. Fixed faith of rich Rome
He'll not open fight on account of his own,
With still other reason, since law doth allow
Man may adore eucharist, or even dun cow.
He'll Protestant be, like nerved, noble North,
Land chiefest in grand deeds that glorify earth.
North nemorous sound is; sloth Southern zone
Servile, artistic, so dreamy in tone,
Hath romantic creed whose grand, mythic features
To paparchy knit impulsive, cringe creatures

Supporting false faith with frail foot in gloom's grave—
Faith able no longer men with mind to enslave;
Faith, therefore, not fatal, but sublime to survey—
Perhaps to revere in sad, slow, sure decay.
Lay Catholic, if true to Apostolic creed,
In goodness none other can ever exceed,
But so dark's papal church, cunning's cloak o'er it spread,
Pope may be fiend foulest—fine hands bloody, red—
Yet in Vatican's bosom in honor repose
Saint such as Richard, who wore withered white rose.
Papal creed theologic, for paradise fit,
Damned is by pope's cunning—by damned Jesuit—
By political part of Rome's crafty see
Whose breath is contagion—e'er blights liberty.
But brave babe here I hold, with spatulate hand,
Tho' he may grant favors to 'postolic band,
Wilt have too much Luther, Jack Calvin, John Knox,
To wrecked ever be against Romish rocks.
This babe man in Scotland, in highland, or low,
Wouldst one time fought fierce for God's faith, felon foe
Crowned villains,soiled oiled queens, laced bastard dukes,
Mitred despots, bench cattle, court curs, jury pukes.
Now your babe I surrender. Despite moon demure,
Whose silver you saw him to-night so allure,
With care—close attention—I predict will arise
His name to adorn, all this globe to surprise."
So saying, old Galen, far famed for his squills,
Large learning, long leeches, keen lancets, prime pills,
Drew on his shag great-coat, month being March rough,
Withdrew, mounted gig, drove away rather gruff,
For father, who out with old Galen didst linger
Grave moment, gave pillbags long, very big finger,
Which then in New Jersey, as elsewhere, was never
So welcome as lucre that lines pliant leather.
Pay cash down on nail; avoid debt obligation;
Then you may find peace, not curst litigation,
Which fattens on debt like caw crow on prone corse
Of lamb, bullock, bison, buck, hart, heifer, horse,
For Bob Holland says—Bob, who often thinks deep—
That man who pays cash is wise man who buys cheap.

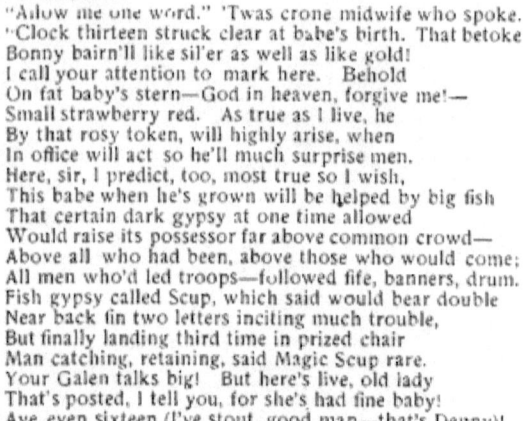

"Allow me one word." 'Twas crone midwife who spoke.
"Clock thirteen struck clear at babe's birth. That betoke
Bonny bairn'll like sil'er as well as like gold!
I call your attention to mark here. Behold
On fat baby's stern—God in heaven, forgive me!—
Small strawberry red. As true as I live, he
By that rosy token, will highly arise, when
In office will act so he'll much surprise men.
Here, sir, I predict, too, most true so I wish,
This babe when he's grown will be helped by big fish
That certain dark gypsy at one time allowed
Would raise its possessor far above common crowd—
Above all who had been, above those who would come;
All men who'd led troops—followed fife, banners, drum.
Fish gypsy called Scup, which said would bear double
Near back fin two letters inciting much trouble,
But finally landing third time in prized chair
Man catching, retaining, said Magic Scup rare.
Your Galen talks big! But here's live, old lady
That's posted, I tell you, for she's had fine baby!
Aye, even sixteen (I've stout, good man—that's Denny)!
While Galen, so learned, huh! never had any!
Sweet baby all right is from topknot to tarse,
But, folks, keep your eye upon mark on fat"—
"Farse!
Nonsense! Stuff! Drivel!" So father shrieked hot,
Dismissing blunt midwife, who spoke as she thought,
Which now's not in fashion. To-day it is style
To converse very clean, though thinking most vile.
Rank, filthy idea, if tinged with Cologne,
Fine ladies delights—is true tonic to tone
Impaired social system, give most fiction zest,
Spice flat repartee, jollify jejune jest.
Poudrette wrap in satin, silk-tassel, perfume,
Behold, it's fair-fingered in wealth's drawing-room!
In parlor, cafe, yacht, boudoir, grand hotel—
Craved solace of beau, lively joy of bold belle.
But drop into Saxon—say only plain "Stink"—
Your name's on pink shell! You, ostracized, sink!
Hence, be ye all guarded—euphemistic, or French;
Descend not to "Stink," nor indulge e'en in "Stench."

But cloak coarse idea in words long, sonorous,
As she's Aphrodite when meaning she whore is;
Then you'll be hailed cultured, wise, polished, pure, clean—
Tongue product untainted, though mind most obscene.
Brisk babe was bright boy. You've seen so already,
But's well to repeat to keep long tale steady,
Which is proper word, strong AS. with kidney—
Used, too, you may find, by Sir Philip Sidney;
By Coleridge, too, or something quite near it;
If you have least doubt, why, damn it, you clear it,
For've had windy leech; also, bouncing baby—
Good Lord, agreed, we'll another have may be;
So've little time to turn analytical,
Hunt you up authors, be squeamish critical.
We're mere reporting, or telling this story,
Which starts rather tame, but winds up in glory;
So often Sol, in clouds all darkling day o'er,
Then welcomes calm night in sea of red splendor.
Now, here's precise place to make free confession:
We beg stickler's pardon for not worst transgression;
Slight regard critics paid, but fashion these verses
Not caring French sou for hacks' praise, or curses,
Critics hired, en herd, being vapid, cheap scoffers
Who rarely e'en equal flat, scurviest authors;
You'll find some exceptions, proving positive rule—
Cheap, average-class critic is egoist fool.
He's telling forever, in oceans of ink,
How McCulloughs should act, profound sages think;
How Pattis should sing, Dante Angelos paint;
How to make devils saints—to better best saint,
When full you may find it's clean, hard, honest fact
Such critic hath naught he raves scored toilers lack;
His mission on earth to hunt faults to berate—
Faults, too, he'll e'er find, tho' them forced to create.
Doth new thing public please? Then people are lewd,
Or coarse; pleaseth not, then, behold, thing is crude!
With little His Highness is pleased to agree;
To applaud would degrade by proving that he
Had found, for great wonder, in world's barren waste,
Some work fully suiting refined, perfect taste.

But there should be true test. Ye Voltaires, forsake
Your pads, pots, bribes, pencils, to please undertake
Control of all arts. Come, mount mimic stage!
Write all valued books—embellish each page;
Preach; paint every canvas; etch, decorate, carve;
Compose—play all music, though harmony starve;
Write song, epic, drama, piece comic, grave, drear—
Be student, creator, instructor, art's Lear!
Let Winter turn Wallack—Willie deign to assume
All roles he hath riddled with shot in Tribune;
Or let him be cast in grand opera role
To howl base or tenor from north to south pole;
Then send him to England to tear-soak green sod—
To wail in grand abbey where wits by square rod
Are sleeping as soundly as song, book, play or jest,
They pen'd with bright hopes,often barbs in man's breast.
Make WeepingWill laureate—present him shoon—shoes—
Proud Tennyson wore when he walked with quaint muse,
Loud wailing in sackcloth since Austin, bard dire,
Repeatedly rapes her when clawing her lyre.
Cast Boston McConnel, along with Nym Crinkle,
With Goodale, wid McPhelin, in "Tom," or "Van Winkle;"
In Greek, Hun, Jew, German, as you have apt notion,
Find something suiting scribe with Inter Ocean;
Role give sapid Johnston, who's critical law,
Condemning, commending, Star-throned, beside Kaw;
Town Topics McLellan might appear as proud Turk,
Or shrewd, canny Scot with kilt, claymore, pouch, dirk;
Vain, fictive Meltzer, once herding with Herl'd,
As Richard would likely bring down cheering world,
As now Meltzer hath done, not world of all men,
But Crook Pulitzer pus of pestiferous pen;
Free Fyles, of sage Sun—Fyles keen, clever fellow—
Draft into deep drama sans Lear, swart Othello;
Vast Hillary Bell, he of Press—with Home Journal—
Let him play your devil, as now, right infernal;
Byrne,Hamlin,VanceThompson—just give 'em jack-boots,
Or cast 'em for parts always taken by supes;
Dale, Davis, Steinberg, J. Ranken, M. Fleming,
(Not Agnes May) we are not here condemning,

But suggest each proud part, as "My Lord, your letter,"
"Your carriage awaits, sir," so on, et cæt'r';
Chicago take in, too, with Eastman, News Amy;
John Eckel, with others, draft into meet drama;
But when giving parts, or 'ranging stage jumble,
Mind Fairbanks, Bill Laffan, renowned Alfred Trumble,
Whose name, slightly changed, would him specially fit
In judgment artistic forever to sit.
Have your last trio, too, besides taking part,
Improve by creations all we best have in art—
Surpass all in Greek, Italian, French, German—
Show all other masters to've been merely vermin;
That Phidias lacked in majestic expression;
Praxiteles show puffed, poor retrogression;
That Michael, Da Vinci, Prince Raphael, Titian,
Have been all along but cheap imposition;
Rembrandt, Flemish Rubens, graced Correggio, too,
Paint them up brown, or in cerulean blue!
Whilst such daubs as Turner, Bierstadt, Holbein, Cole,
Old Josh with all Spaniards, just make hunt their hole!
Forget not those critics who music enhance—
Who decide what is low—what doth so entrance;
Who can tell when they hear, or somehow divine,
What's false from what's true, what's coarse, what is fine—
Distinguish, indeed, quick hornpipe, Mick jig,
From festive fandango, or opera big;
Can tell en un tris, so finely they feel,
When kettledrum sounds, or stained violins squeal;
If tuba's in tune; if shrill piccolo's drunk;
By soft note if flute may take out restrained trunk;
Who know all of music from Bach to Beethoven,
From Handel, Strauss, Mozart, to patch-work De Koven,
Who's now—ye gods, weep!—part of tail to foul kite
Joe Magyar from sewer sails bold before sight.
De Koven, Schwab, Krebiel, with great Mr. Finck,
With Henderson, too, Ben Woolf who throws ink
In old Boston so brainy, high-talented band,
Rig up to perform in loud opera grand;
Have them, too, compose, to delight every age,
Each piece they adorn by their art on world's stage.

Roles you also select, very best within reach,
For Hazeltine, Stoddard, bright Brander, bland Beach,
Great quartette with talent enough to supply
All books nations need, or all we should buy,
Of ballads, art, physic, sea, poetry, diction,
History, law, travel, carving, jests, fiction;
For we're reading too much: or, speaking quite true,
Read nearly all books when should study best few.
Colonel Lease wants but three—her list we adduce:
Almighty God's Bible, Shakespeare, Mother Goose.
So Elizabeth says, but she must make mistake,
For she's ink sinned, herself, with quill lucubrate,
Whilst chances are even she's read offense o'er
Not once, twice, or thrice, but times full many score.
But here we disgress. Dismissing Pop lady,
Return to keen critics, then again to fine baby:
Teach each one his part; drill well; full rehearse
Every act, striking scene, splendid speech, motion, verse;
Knit them well in their parts; keep, too, their brains clear
From that Thespian nectar, inspiring beer.

Then, Lord, let them loose! But let them, Art, touch
No part in poor stuff taste trained loves so much,
But have combined troupe with consummate care
Each master-piece staging, or acting, prepare.
Let no artist stoop so low down's to appear
In Hearne, Bulwer, Goldsmith, Crebillon, Shakespeare.
Be, also, impartial. To slight never doom
One critical planet born to blaze away gloom;
But give every critic—Tom, Richard, Harry—
Savants deep most journals pay board for, or carry—
Wig, buskin, motley, harp, palette, chisel,
Gown, mitre, sword—then, then see 'em fizzle!

How all earth, or this half, from foam down to dregs,
Wouldst yell loud "Police!"—wouldst corner up eggs!
There'd be such contention, war, massacre, riot,
That all of Sam's troops could ne'er hope to quiet.
Bartholomew's murders would pale as new day
Compared with vast killing in such mad melee.
Then Art, face in mantle, beholding dread death—
Each favorite slaughtered—wouldst yield her last breath.
But babe needs attention. Brave, lustier lad
Bier Dutch, Scotch, wild Irish, tough Welsh, never had.

Tucked snug in silk kerchief, babe doughty they found
When weighed on steelyard kicked twenty-five pound.
Fact notable, father, with pride, sat to write—
In Bible proceeded to careful indite—
Along with babe's sex—with all information
Befitting notation of such rare addition.
Few babes have weighed more. But one we recall,
Fine twenty-six pounder, pink monster to haul
From dark prison of flesh, that pulsing, quick tomb
From which all resurrect—maternity's womb.
Stout baby Jumbo, by name famed as Bates,
Had parents gigantic who traveled Sam's states;
Through Europe also, with mild "Prince" who declared
Men love to be humbugged: hence, Barnum well-fared,
But humbugged so kindly prompt memory dwells,
Lingering long fondly when tongue, or pen, tells
How him thousands cheered—huzzaed as he went
With proud few favored dead-heads to "acres of tent."
But this is no circus—no place to display
Once splendors of Barnum, now all passed away,
Alas, like himself, with rare wonders—Tom Thumb,
Big Chang of Cathay, loud calliope, drum,
Birds, beasts, vile reptiles—these latter we believe
Directly descended from cuss who caught Eve. [cheer
Yet wouldst dwell with gay circus—here tell what wild
Hosts gave when Old Humbug was proclaimed to appear;
How godly ring-master, with wave, voice aroar,
Wouldst declare, "Greatest wonder! Another! One more!
But I'll not employ words. Here praise is no use!
But Barnum, supremest, himself introduce!"
Talk about cheering! Men, women, babes, boys,
Then ripped up wide welkin with thunderous noise,
Whilst Barnum'd arise, pleased survey intent throng
Wild tumult of plaudits—royal welcome—prolong.
But silence ensuing—dead hush so profound
Oft followeth rain, or hallows fresh mound
As sexton with mattock, moist shovel, or spade,
Goes, leaving hearts broken with icy one laid
In earth cruel, cold—Prince Humbug wouldst speak,
He then beaming god, but full thanks mostly Greek,

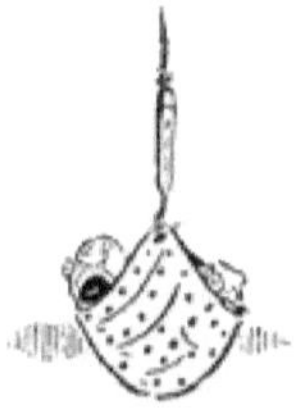

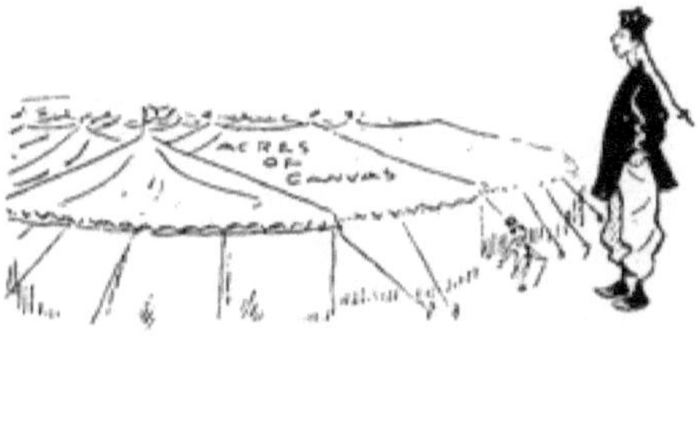

Canvas Cæsar, like Grant, being more for parade
Than cabinet, forum. But we've too much delayed;
So return to our muttons. If you but recur
Just page or so back you'll find we refer
To parent of babe recording great weight,
Sex, date, with so on to keep history straight,
Which would have saved time—made some people know
more—
Had same been performed at moot advent of Homer,
Whose verses today certain papers adduce,
Preferring his old to what new we produce
With other live bards who oft find it rather
Hard to keep souls with spare bodies together,
In face of hard fact great Homer, deceased,
Needs never such comforts at all large or least.
Most manifest outrage! Sense holds prudent state
Should suppress all bards old that new pale may get bait.
It's God's honest fact, certain bards, hunger's prey,
As poor as Job's turkey, can't make verses pay
Unless Boks who publish are swerved to full sense
Of low, biased judgment—mad, mean preference.
We more than suggest. We firm urge, appeal, beg,
Old, dead bards put down, your new poor up one peg.
But, friend, to resume. Keep we on digressing
We'll never get through with facts we are dressing.
After weighing, fond father gray quill solemn took,
Then drew from high shelf big, good, holy book,
In which he recorded hour, day, exact date,
With sex, pregnant portent, likewise immense weight.
To names then they all gave attention devoted,
Considering light ones, odd, sacred, apt, noted.
Celt nurse wanted Pathrick; staunch Democrat, Van,
Who just at that time was most mighty big man,
As he'd been elected to shoulder all care
With honors attending executive chair.
But what of Van now? Nigh forgotten Dutch name!
Stained epitaph largely full meed of great fame!
But babe then in cradle colossal now stands
Fond idol of Mugwumps, oft theme of brass bands!
So singular doom is! No wonder men late
Hath deigned very often to delve into fate,

But wonder is greater that fatalists grow
In number so few—so remarkably slow;
For doom is firm ruler, though it's truth complete,
As Colonel Crisp says, "Men of destiny's cheap."
He's colonel who found—very hotly didst spurn—
On floor once in state house "base human tape-worm."
Crisp's aim on earth highest, with his fondest wish,
Is to cultivate carp with other food fish;
He one time declared, as hitched up ample breeches,
"We all are sad lot of Sax. sons of bitches!"
For Colonel Crisp's plain, likewise at times coarse,
But so was Queen Bess, who was fain to enforce
Her regal commands in rude way rather rash
With language today prudes print with fool ——.
But after debating, at times with no reason,
Folks settled at last on your sainted name Stephen.
They gave babe another, for names are so plenty
Sure one is no cheaper than nineteen or twenty.
But moment's digression. It was bard's intention
To give batch of names debaters didst mention;
To dwell for few moments on each in long list,
Detailing full meaning, but we must desist.
Yet here recommend you consult Proverb Tupper,
Whom some folks still read.
Bold babe once at supper,
His months being six then, also having pluck,
Surprised all at table by calling out "Duck!"
Which from his high chair valiant baby had seen
As bird stuck his legs up in wide, white tureen.
Now Steve from that day as babe, man, blooming boy,
Fat duck of all fowls ever found his chief joy.
He thus early, too, once raised frightful storm
For "revenue only," with "tariff reform,"
But growing still older, more certain inclined
To politics pure, which thrived much in rich mind.
Diderot, with such like, babe had in chaste cradle;
On Cobbett—on Story—he oft gorged at table
With physics, philosophy, hist'ry, old ballad,
Along with his taters, tea, turnips, salad.
But not as we study, or pick up, or read,
With such infinite care. No, no! No, indeed!

Lore he simply absorbed. Through pores in soft skin
He took immense quantum of politics in
With all other learning. He sat on Voltaire,
Then straightway talked French beyond all compare.
So, too, with Latin, Greek, New Jersey, Hebrew—
He mastered them all as easy as we do
Sit down in cane chair, on soft sofa, or street
When ice isn't salted—when we fail on our feet;
On Cæsar, Virgil, Homer, Luther, bold Locke,
Babe spent but two hours, nurse declar'd, watching clock.
Bacon, Burke, Bonaparte, Copernicus, Cato,
Socrates, Solomon, Seneca, Plato,
Sam Johnson, Sappho, Plutarch, Pliny, Solon,
He absorbed in one day as each he didst roll on;
Pat Henry's speeches, Ben Franklin, Gay, Milton,
Complete got by heart just with slightest tilt on.
As crawled on oak floor, odd, marvelous creature
On Bible old fell, then knew more than preacher.
Ovid, Lycurgus, Livy, Ossian, Zeno,
He learned in one day. Too very well we know,
For it's fairly recorded, all written out plain,
How Sallust, like Xenophon, reached baby's brain.
Pope, Spenser, Shakespeare, Swift, with "rare Ben,"
He absorbed at short sitting. Damned accident then,
Or shortly thereafter, we're not splitting hairs,
Complete changed bright aspect of babe's book affairs.
Babe ate with keen relish. He seemed child annoyed
With clamorous, aching, n'er-filled inner void.
So great Ouida tells us your dirty Italian
Is far more omnivorous than starving battalion;
For, so she says, to him all is edible—
What he will eat is simply incredible.
Italia herself, Abyssinia's salet,
Is now absolutely without any palate—
Steeps hares in fennel—yea, worse than all Hellens—
Salt languidly eats with cucurbit'ous melons.
From Alps on to Ætna 'tis said all are crazy
For small birds as well as most damnably lazy.
There's species of frenzy, without seeming cause,
To craunch small birds' bodies twixt very strong jaws

With relish disgusting. But most succulent morsel
Is sweet little lark, whose foes deserve coarse hell—
In fact, worse than painted by popes, divine Dante,
For glory of God, as we're willing to grant ye.
Enormous, it's said, while certain most sable,
Is round-up for larks for Epicure's table.
All over earth, so it seems—they admit it—
They crave lark for pasties, or are savage to spit it.
In England this slaughter goes on as near Rome;
All over Gaul worse than we here at home;
Then there's awful fear if slaughter goes on,
This trapping, vile vending, vast eating, ere long
There'll not be sweet lark to soar up in thin air.
In fact, it is feared, soon all birds may be rare—
Not only lark songsters, killed one at sad time,
But whole tribes extinct, thinning science calls crime.
You know of great auk? Well, he, arctic, 's no more,
But gone to fair av'ry on other far shore.
He was not flying bird, but built on squat plan
Of Dutch jug, or demijohn, still much used by man.
Auk's wings were but stumps; he'd sit squat on his rear;
He in such position looked quite as severe
As judge grave, or bishop. Each foot had thin web;
Foot shoved he in tide's flow—also worked in ebb.
Blond Swedes called him alka, but in Hebrew, Hun, Swede,
Great auk is no more—extinct's bizarre breed,
Which many regret, for without awkward auk
Who knows but great danger may assail tariff talk!
But though great auk is out, still have we marrot,
Called puffin also, pope, murre, sea-parrot;
If that's not enough, then still have we pug
With pert curl in cauda, with monkey-like mug.
So let us all trust in joy Ouida may rest
Though every bird's slaughtered, destroyed's every nest.
Your terrier, or pug, of course, cannot sing
Like saccharose songsters in cage, swift awing,
But terrier with pug makes up for all that
By mussing up baby, or tumbling up cat
As if, you'd imagine, concupiscent cur
Had taken lewd notion to violate her,

Or carry her hence, as bold Romans succeeded
With Sabines fair when wives Romans needed,
Which was too heroic, but similar fate
Almost prevails now—there's legalized rape,
As Harman well knows, for Harman they jugged
For scoring some brutes for way they fierce hugged.
Prime, principal point in that case as seen is
Good Moses in paper put what rhymes with Venus,
Which jurors, with judge, declared wasn't legal
Though very best Latin by Virgil, Ast, Schlegel—
Word noted by Noah in his bulky book,
As you may have seen, for it's legal to look.
But Moses to durance, though aged, dolts sent,
Not for lewd insertion, but lethal intent,
Which may be good law, for glad babe in pure glee
May show in all candor what were quite wrong in thee;
Fair thought, you may know, that is none of our own,
But great Mr. Fielding's to defend tainted tome.
Thus, you see, we give credit, at least to some men,
Which isn't late practice 'mong most wielding pen,
As were easy to prove; we need but refer
To fine Lady Mary with fine wits about her.
But it makes little odds; to us matters not,
Though hell is to pay with no pitch in smudge pot.
Quick babe, as we said—on this page plain repeat—
Was monster to learn, greedy monster to eat,
But went rather far. You know how success
Leads many great men into fatal excess.
Napoleon, remember; Oil Creek Johnny Steel,
With thousands of others whose names we could reel
Here off in two minutes, but must firm resist
Such pleasing temptation—must grind out gross grist,
Which we've too much neglected to loiter at will
In woods, dingles, meadows, on way to old mill.
But beaten road's hard! It's so dull—O, so long!
Whilst byways, green woodlands, all beauty, all song,
Invite, call, allure us with flowers, birds, brooks—
Sometime, too, dead silence. But now to grave books,
To babe, damned disaster—calamitous close
Of marvelous gift—brightest hopes that arose

In father's heart happy. It happened this way—
Please pardon false grammar: Blithe nursemaid one day,
Careless slut that she was, to cure baby's phthisic,
Gave him Culpeper with Galen on physic,
Hoping, said she in her rich Irish tone,
"To shure kill two burds with but one single sthone,"
Which surely she did, for deep works were so large,
Contained so much physic—that poor girl's discharge
Immediate followed. Wondrous babe nevermore
Absorbed Greek, nor Latin, nor aught, on oak floor!
Complete was ruth ruin. No learning remained;
Culpeper proved fatal; how, shan't be explained,
For there are occasions when language doth fail;
Also, certain scenes virtue begs men to veil.
'Twas fell blow for father so expectant to bear—
His hopes rudely shattered—gone all up in air;
Expensive, as well, for glad father had bought
Big cartload of tomes of clean, very best thought
For babe to absorb, when, lo, friend, behold,
Nurse acts giddy fool—there woe deep, untold!
He'd Jefferson, Jackson, Monroe, Newton, Pitt,
Exact Lord Macaulay with few books of wit,
For father was wise, holding all men should read
"Very much," so he said, "as your best people feed."
Some prefer what's profound, but you'll find most remain
Where wit is bubbling—with crisp lines in light vein.
Juicy joint we enjoy, but still palate wishes
Figs, walnuts, red wine, spiced, dainty side dishes.
We may affect thinkers who ever ask "Why?"
But turn for relief to tart Dana, mourned Nye,
Puck, Judge, Life, Truth, rare, alluring Town Topics;
Keen Pixley yet, too; Field—Eugene, with tuned tropics;
Or, go to hear Ingersoll who forces to cheers,
So perfectly blends he light laughter with tears.
Indeed, grin at Talmage, that spectacular man
Who's found quite as taking as ever old Van,
Whose circus you saw, perhaps, years ago
When Hannibal swayed with tough Tip in small show.
So we go to hear Jones—motley Sam—just as soon—
As eager as pay to applaud gross buffoon.

Mountebank in God's pulpit! Coarse clown in church cloth
Who'd lead us to Jesus with jest, guffaw, scoff!
So bright babe grew apace, as all babies should,
Hale, fat, happy, hearty, to lusty boyhood,
Then forth went to school; there he grew very wise,
Surpassing deep master in each exercise,
Rude rustics surprising, as once did mild sage
Whom Goldsmith declares could actually gauge.

Our hero was fine. He was large for his years—
Good eyes, nose, mouth, forehead—significant ears.
These latter mean much, though they spread like belle's fan
Sticking out, or close cling to head of your man.
His ear was not vast, but was betwixt, or between—
True medium, rather, or ear golden-mean.
Those hairs there protective, adhesive with wax,
'Twas noticed were silver. We state these small facts
That you may conclude by judging from face,
Or boy's head, with parts all we'll soon fully trace,
If youth may excel, be candid, close, jealous—
Grow up to be great, or end on crime's gallows.
You've seen Patti's ear? Well, when he was young,
Steve's much was like her's—fair queen's! She hath sung
Delighting dull earth. When she goes up above
She'll lead heaven's choir. Eager angels will shove—
Aye, crowd to get closer—all over her wing
To thrill, amaze, marvel, applaud when she'll sing.

As we've not seen her lately, have asked for no gear,
No coin, we submit our poor praise is sincere,
For which we take credit, for critics now'days
Are prone to abuse, or to fulsomely praise,
As refuse, or accede, you to pay down on nail,
Or take them as equals. Hence, bribes so prevail
You rarely can tell till you use ears, or eyes,
If critique is plain truth, or libel of lies.
But lug we neglect, not alert of dun deer,
Timid mouse, rat, or cat, but human, so here:
Skilled authors declare, so shrewdly didst delve,
Distinctive-type ears number evenly twelve,
As Singer, Commercial, Vulgar, Artistic,
Murderer, Miser, your Cautious one mystic,

Benevolent, Thief, ear Perfect, Mechanic,
With Musical ear very keenly tympanic.
Your ear of fine singer hath bell deeply fluted—
Is long, also narrow, or so is reputed.
Your eyra commercial is thick, heavy, massive;
Large ear of Dan Drew be sure in this class have.
Vulgar ear—you have seen it—mean, clumsy, thick,
All fleshy, lobe heavy, making cultured taste sick;
But ear of true artist is pink as sea shell,
Is long, thin—is fluted remarkably well,
Like ear Richard Mansfield is said to possess—
Your symmetrical ear, as savants know or guess.
Then blood-thirsty ear—broad, fleshy thing—shallow
In fluting is his who killeth his fellow.
Pale miser's is thick—flat also—'tis said
Almost without fluting to cling close to head.
Such ears, Mr. Wells says, rich Astors display,
As also Jew Rothschilds. Your cautious ears stay
Close rather to caput—are broad, too, at top,
With lobe that is narrow, as oft in fool fop.
Benevolent ears are large—democratic,
As small are supposed to be 'ristocratic,
Ear former in fluting being found very deep,
Hencé distinct. Benefactors, who feel when we weep,
Have often ears large with other large parts—
Large feet with large hope, large hands with large hearts,
As Cooper, as Mason, as Garrison, Hopper,
Abe Lincoln, Grange Greeley. There's also your lop-ear.
Coarse ear of sly thief has inconformable rim;
Is thick, heavy, flat, or they lie about him.
Well-rounded, thin, soft, pink, elastic, quite clear,
Is what's called Apollo's, or perfect-formed, ear.
Mechanical ear is broad about middle,
Like ladies sometimes, but never fine fiddle.
Very delicate-rounded is rim of nice ear,
Broad-fluted, deep, pink, so delighting to hear
Sounds grand, sonorous—ear musical named—
Pole Paderewski's, we recall, it is claimed.
Not one of these ears, we so careful describe,
Belonged to small Steve, but his pair were full pride

Of nascent New Jersey, so famous for years
For cranberry marshes, mosquitoes, fruit, ears.
But so much for auris, odd thing complicated;
We return to Steve's eyes, to nose close related,
So Franklin declared; quaint Ben we allow
Wot all that he wrote, as we think we wot now.
Boy's eyes were not Tasso's, for Tasso's were wild;
But Steve's were now fierce—again pensively mild;
Their color we give not, for hue of all eyes
Is less worthy notice than motion with size,
For fools you may find with black, brown, gray or blue,
Green, flecked with hazel—every other eye hue,
But, judging by hair, his ancestors, good birth,
Marked bent of rich mind, right conduct, high worth,
His eye was gray-green, or just really reverse—
Sort of Joan-of-Arc eye—maid Cath'lics didst curse,
She feeding fierce flames—sure very brave deed,
But comporting in France at that time with monks' creed.
His orbs were alert—indeed, some relate,
In Emerson's words, he had "eye full of fate;"
Not so large as Nell Gwynn's, nor Helen's of Troy,
Nor Lola-Montes orbs to move, charm, decoy.
His eyes stood not out like optics of crab,
Gazelle or antelope, but yet were not bad,
Deep-seated, nor small, as you see in sty pig,
But just full enough, not too small, nor too big;
Not widely-expanded—round-formed—as in owls
That hoot in night's gloom—so fancy fat fowls.
His eye wasn't downcast, nor yet "upward glancing,"
Like those of madonnas, or maids mad romancing;
Nor wonder-filled either, nor too deeply sunken,
Nor "wrapped in devotion," nor laughing, nor drunken,
But every-day eye found in Yankee, Swedes, Scots,
Cold English, hot Irish, in saints, in some sots.
His eye being light it were easy to trace
He was one of nice youths of most civilized race,
For climate doth tend to give your eye hue—
Eye tropical dark, North light—perhaps blue;
But to sum it all up, both eyes of Fat Knight,
As he turned out to be, were just about right.

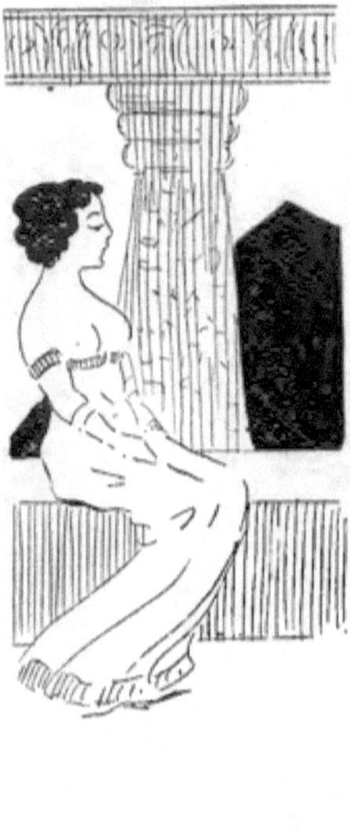

They were not Cleopatra's voluptuous, slack,
Nor Aspasia's gray, nor de Medici's black,
Beautiful, crafty, cold, cruel, ne'er tender—
Of whom it is written "She had all * * * splendor"
That's found in dread tiger. What pity that fate
Deprived these New Women of having great Kate
To lead them—to counsel—to give them best plan
To humble—deep trample in earth brutal man!
So much for Steve's eye. It is pertinent now
To glance just above it—to read Stephen's brow,
Which should never be done if you find subject's eye
Is abraded, or darkened, or swollen, or spy
Brown bee, fierce hornet, mad wasp, yellow-jacket,
Red brick, made for orb—didst fierce, fell attack it,
For if you decide from form so extraneous,
Why, ten to one, you'll conclude erroneous.
As you may have observed—in fact, apt detected—
All eyes to eyebrows are quite closely connected,
Not only in place, but also in action,
Expression, cast, so on, like party to faction.
Man's brow may be thick, may be thin, coarse or fine,
Smooth, bushy, arched, or straight as true line,
But brow plainly thick—some experts call it strong—
Is generally dark—to France doth belong,
As once we discovered when chancing to look
Into "New Physiognomy," wise, excellent book
For ministers, poets, limners, e'en sages—
Great work of some hundred clean, well-printed pages—
Teaching how to take ear, eye, lip, hand, or toe,
Heart, hair, or incisor, then whole corpus know.
Such work, we opine, if we'll understood,
If heeded, would lessen divorces—it should.
Take eyebrow, for instance. All ifs, with all buts,
All small, subtle facts, with fine lot of clear cuts,
Tome places before you. Make book all your own,
Get flesh with red blood of it—skin, sinew, bone—
Then take satisfaction in walking in street,
Close reading all faces—all forms—you may meet,
For it beats auction-pitch. Good brow of bright boy,
According with hand, ear, mouth, eye, gave joy
To doctor—fond father—who beheld in boy's brow,

As if mirrored there, success vast, that now
Embalmed is historic, or shalt ever be
When this is complete—Knight's full history.
This but introductory, initial, first,
Just paving work's way, being, also, part worst;
This mere how-are-you act, nigh lifeless; but magic,
March, havoc, war, blood, hell, end drama tragic,
Gore-soaked, horrific.
Steve's brow slight didst lower,
Full, dead-certain proof of command—awful power.
Straight also was Steve's brow; likewise was it dark,
But not quite so ebon as crow in pitched ark.
Boy's peach cheek was round—quite smooth as fair
forehead—
Which, at that time, was not coarse, nor florid,
But grew so on later—not owing to breeding,
But calm, close attention to drinking, deep feeding.
But it might more instruct this order to stop—
To begin with Steve's feet, or commence at tiptop,
Or e'en maiden middle, in babyhood trim
But later, by all gods, part mainest of him!
We'll begin, then, with dome, or crown flat, of head,
First touching lad's hair, then abundantly spread—
Fine, silky in texture—that time darkish brown,
All over Steve's caput, from nape up to crown,
We briefly depicting, as sketch we complete,
Each feature from head to soles, sensate, of feet;
So, when all is said, if any way clever,
We'll have quite French Trilby, or fine, "altogether,"
Omitting, of course, in true sketch to include
Anything not approved by men pious, or prude.
So then to hair silky. Fat Knight's, in his youth,
Was thick, deep, dark brown, but now, to tell truth,
Is thin, crisp, quite coarse—aye, is falling away,
Which, some men stout assert, means mental decay.
It may not be believed, but his hair displayed scales,
Like those on fishes, but never on whales,
Very much like odd crop that Wulferus found
All over dread corpse many years under ground.
Steve's hair wasn't parted amiddle like Dante's,
But color of crop was close like Cervantes's,

That kind that prevails as set, general rule,
In hot, Southern countries; light hair's in lands cool,
Or latitude temperate, but yet, it is noted,
Your heads in close cities are usually coated
With thatch that is dark. Steve combined in brown hair
All taste of South dark with all strength of North fair.
Having kind most desired. His hair never fell
In length like long locks of mad men who rebel,
But was cropped rather close,like Heenan's,tough Sayers's,
Jim Corbett's, Fitz's, John's, or other short-hairs's.
Of course it was straight, plain fact indicating,
If mind of hair wearer has had cultivating,
Fair character even, clear head, with good talents,
While golden, or red, goes most with loose gallants.
Lucrezia, who poisoned in age rather olden,
We're told, by Lord Byron, had locks purely golden.
So'd Helen of Troy, so Sylla, so Tasso,
With whole raft of others we've no time to class. Oh,
How great we regret fleet time's ever pressing!
Wouldst it but stand still, or turn back, ever blessing!
But it goes with mad rush—goes ever amain—
Us bidding proceed. We come now to Steve's brain.
Disdaining to stop to dwell keen, or dull,
On plates, or those bones, of knowledge-box, skull,
Except to remark that head of our hero
Resembled his neck, not long like Fah. zero,
We find head broad, short, strong, not greatly unlike
Yankee Sullivan's nut he bade students strike;
Steve's caput comported remarkably neat
With all from flat crown to wide soles of fat feet.
He had plenty of brain, but not much vivacity,
But stability, force, with right good capacity;
His compact brain was bulky, which made him emphatic;
His temper most cold, or mixed, sangui-phlegmatic,
Or, as some say, quite vital, so frequently found
With bulged abdomen large, short neck, with face round.
His forehead was broad, but not so capacious
As Bacon's, or Byron's, or we're not veracious.
He had Grecian nose, but it doesn't follow
His organ of scent was perfect Apollo,

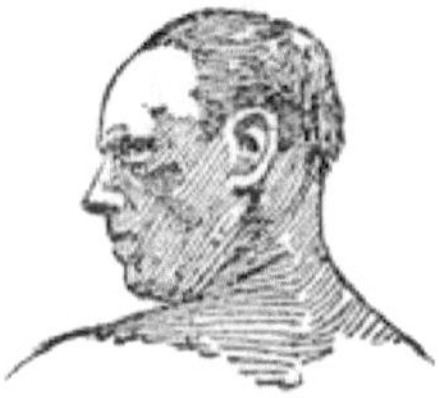

But had it well-trained, for such his keen smell
He could any liquid distinguish, or tell;
Nay, not only that, but would he engage,
By smelling of whisky, to give exact age.
With same nasal organ he'd pick out pure flock
Of future reformers, locate scented sock,
Trace game, as otter, hare, deer, marmot, mink,
Muskrat or weasel, by well-defined stink.
By nose he'd determine just where he was at;
He had no superior at smelling brown rat.
Men also observed as he grew greater, old,
By smelling alone he found good, yellow gold,
Odd new way to prospect, or locate ore mine,
But better by far than in rude '49.
His nose was aggressive; it made him quite willing
To trudge many miles for less than York shilling,
Which fact we commend, for wise men must consent
Cold cash, or its worth, is true root of content.
Stern mouth was Stephen's; 'twas nigh straight across;.
His chin was good-sized one, as oft seen in joss;
His neck large in youth, but much thicker in age,
Being then like prize bull's, seen seldom in sage;
So large, ribald wits declared Stephen should wear
Stiff collar of leather for stallion, or mare.
Steve's neck gladiatorial completed stiff spine
Stout, tough as hick'ry, as straight as Scotch pine;
That is, in Steve's youth, but years, as they flew,
Showed plainly sag curve from posterior view.
Broad, ample his chest, as in age his great girth,
Affording small Raymonds much occasion for mirth,
Full many scrubs penning he'd surely surpass
In waist-band endowment famed Sir Hudibras.
In age bulk before matched great bulk behind,
Latter out-jutting, but eclipsed by vast mind.
So Butler, of knight, doth short-measured relate;
Sam's wit just above we insert 'propriate.
Steve's young legs were trim—in fact, neater pair
Pantaloons never covered, nor were seen ever bare..
Forth-coming reformer, to make him complete,
Attached to trim legs had clean pair of prime feet.

Which thrived as he throve—as each other part
Waxed buttock, grew girth, his hands, his head, heart.
When less than fifteen, trade deep to explore,
Behold, you find Stephen installed in small store
Where close Jersey farmers, stout matrons, coy maid,
With butter, eggs, other stuff, called in to trade.
There Ben Davis apples, potatoes sweet, beans,
Pork, turnips, beets, oft exchanged were for jeans.
Wool also was haggled, farm's staple connection
Infecting bright youth with "pizen" protection,
That very vexed theme, one time heard contin'ly,
Displaying for years full depth of McKinley.
Thus, adolescent, high tariff's Steve's hobby,
As subsequent platforms, still later rank lobby
So saccharine, teeming—so senatorial,
Rich, potent, placid, knave, dictatorial.
Steve sold suspenders, fur hats, gloves, spice, tidies—
To young mothers stuff to make babies "didies:"
Sold carpets, bed-ticking, "working pants," matting,
Tobacco, snuff, shirts, thread, overalls, batting,
Washtubs, boots, shoes, black pepper, salt, nutmegs,
Codfish, red herring, gut fiddlestrings, shoe pegs,
Beef dried, choice lard, snaps, crackers, Young Hyson,
Sardines, new brooms, tea, coffee, bug "pizen,"
Soap, sugar, cider, cheese, clams, pickles, honey,
Scrub-brushes, tar, pots—in trade or for money.
They kept in large stock for tramp, or rich banker,
All manner of goods from needle to anchor.
In that mart—emporium—so varied, full-freighted,
Steve learned immense deal—grew wide educated,
Insight keen getting there into all classes,
Men, worldly manners, salt fish, fruit, molasses,
Wisdom plain aiding to make him unconquer'ble—
Out in wide world Knight insurmountable!
Steve made splendid record, his fame spreading wide—
In store, village, farm-house, they hailed him with pride.
Though stipend was small, full round year remained he,
Trade hoping to master—shrewd merchant to trained be.
But "No!" thundered doom. Yet, despite his poor pay,
In store in New Jersey might Steve been today

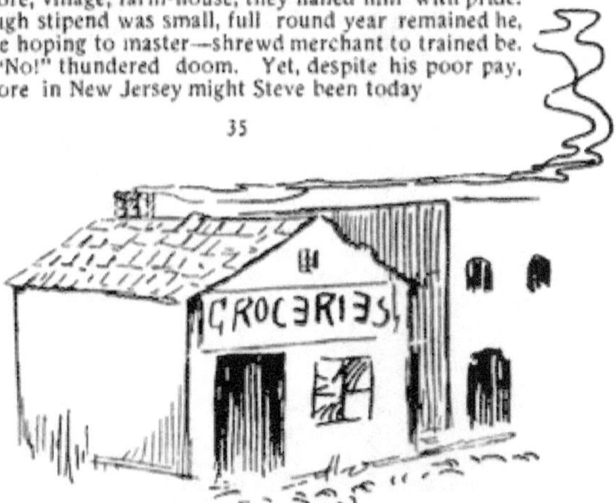

Had not fell disaster, by hate hatched, alas!—
It certain was fate, so singular pass—
Relentless in fury invested that boy,
Implacable bent Stephen poor to destroy.
His temper was mild, but yet Stephen was firm;
He'd stand very much, yet wilt earthworm e'en turn.
Though not any stuck up, 'twas plain manly youth,
Who, in all justice, was not then uncouth,
Felt his oats, as they say—was proud of his knowledge,
Not as vain peacock, nor puffed ass from college,
But pleased very well with all he well knew,
Which, we confess, was quite pretty store, too,
For boy of fifteen. He used to make speeches
At that very time—right roundly roast "leeches
Now sucking our life-blood!"—unanswerable phrase
Vast tickling close farmers, gaining lad pleasing praise.
Now, it chanced Steve'd fell foe. Dark, bony, lank,
Unscrupulous devil—cold, full-blooded Yank,
Who envied bright boy—base resolved to scheme low
To humiliate deep lad brave at one blow,
Which, damn him, he did! Lank, dark, bony cuss
Not only did that, but raised malign muss
All 'round there in Jersey. Now, Steve wore his shoes,
His pantaloons, also, remarkably loose,
Not only for comfort, but allow ample room
So all his quick parts could ramify—boom.
It chanced Stephen's tailor had made his last pair
Of trousers far bigger than lad was aware.
Out behind breeches stuck for fully three feet—
In all of New Jersey none had seen such vast seat.
In front ample, too; stout wool stuff was loud;
So folks to see breeches rushed in in great crowd,
Plain fact lad construed to mean laughing men,
Fat matrons, coy maidens, wouldst have him speak. Then
Out to great common broad, Steve, glad, leading way,
They went very merry—that full seat made them gay.
Arriving, Steve mounted barrel once finest flour
Had filled; then harangued 'em for fully half hour,
When dark, lean cuss bony slipped up in boy's rear,
Seat cutting away, causing shirt to appear.

Now seat was so wide, devilish scamp worked so well,
Warmed speaker knew not when disaster befel,
But fervent declaimed, whilst wide out in gale,
West wind blowing some, flapped Stephen's shirt-tail.
When outrage was finished—ended rape fell of breech—
Coarse Jerseymen howled; many Jersey maids' screech
Was heard full long mile; but some blushed as red
As nose of old toper, or turkey-cock's head.
But lad thundered loud on; gave many thrust
To goldbug, to Wall street, greed's corner, curst trust;
We give not his words, but tell what he meant,
As eloquent grew he, with white shirt out rent,
Whilst farmers old howled yet louder—roared, cheered,
Tho' some Jersey maidens had then disappeared.
Brave, eloquent boy, with very good cause,
Mistaken had reason for cheers, wild applause.
He might have gone on had not greater woe,
In figure as fact, truly laid him down low.
Base miscreant lank, with raped seat on long pole,
In rear of young speaker very stealthily stole,
Then raised high torn emblem. Then lad cast his eye
From faces before him to hell's outrage on high.
Divining damned truth, in anger—red shame—
He reached for long pole, but missed mangled game,
For just at that moment, old barrel-head, so weak,
Gave way with loud crash, whilst Steve, like jagged streak
Of lightning that blanches ere thunderous sound,
Sped through flour barrel down—down to hard ground!
Descending through barrel, curved part that prevails
In rear of mankind encountered sharp nails.
Yet lad didn't whimper. But swore he could "lick
Damned scoundrel who did such low, dirty trick!"
Securing rent seat, he pinned it with care
To place it belonged with grave, undaunted air:
But his heart was full sore; in his young burning soul
There surged mighty sea of bitterest dole;
He swore in his anguish he'd shake from his feet
Dust of town so debased as to attack urchin's seat.
Repairing to store, he packed up, then drew
What wage he had coming—to some said adieu;

Then went to his lodging. His merchant career
There ended forever.
It is oftentimes queer
What small things determine what mortals shall be;
How they one lad affected kind reader may see,
If patient to follow—with us to pursue
Brave hero we'll trace till we're quite with him through,
Or, rather, till he is through with base earth—.
This narrative reaches from time of babe's birth
Till you come to hic jacet; in fact, men, indeed,
It may some bit farther than that e'en proceed,
For we have full right with Dante to tell,
Or Milton, all wonders of heaven or hell,
In one of which regions, if religion's but true,
You may find our hero when you pass away, too.
Kind merchant was raging when heard he how lad
Was outraged when speaking. In truth it was sad.
Those farmers in Jersey denied they had meant
To see Stephen harmed—they'd no evil intent,
But confes'd when damn'd rogue, with winks, with sly leers,
Essayed operations on seat with big shears,
They'd felt too amused, or amazed, to oppose—
They had nothing to do, they declared, with lad's clothes.
They were conservative men—they cared not to mix
Very much with deep subject of complex politics.
Name of rogue who offended they would not reveal,
Despite every threat—despite best appeal,
But many years after, when many who roared
That day at base crime had been called to blessed Lord,
Full truth came to light, when't started fierce feud
That threatened full often to cause sea of blood,
Admonishing all who this history peruse
Never seat rights of others to wanton abuse.
Red spark kindles blaze that fanned by light wind
May wipe out vast city. Through sneers men have sinned
Most damnably deep. Fickle, scandalous breath,
Perhaps half in jest, hath wrought feuds sowing death.
Hence, men, be ye careful. Disdain to stand by
Mute, seeing black outrage; ne'er, men, utter lie,
But, men, for God's sake, for honor, for riches,
See never rogue rip rear of any man's breeches!

For what, let us ask, is more sacred than clothes
That cover parts carnal we should not expose?
Ham's stripping beat treason! Those who foul offend
In any such wise should grace gallows rope's end!
This subject, we know, is not easy to touch
Without saying too little, or attempting too much,
But demands stern attention, which here we essay
Before to next canto, or book, we away.
Before we go thence, to begin second part,
We wish to allude to some nude found in art.
Such works as "Love's Prisoner," on calendars found,
All country should shock—must surely astound,
Displaying fine female, with magnificent bust,
With never one rag on, to stimulate lust,
Surrounded by Cupids, by boys' fronts, alack!
With not single stitch to plump belly or back!
Can you wonder at cyclones, tornadoes, wrecks, storms!
That tramps roam at large in this country in swarms
Like locusts in Egypt! That, bending in woe,
In Gotham is Comstock—chaste Antonio!
It's infamous, shocking! But even base nude
In world artistic is not nearly so rude,
Nor outrage di'bolic as one perpetrated
When lad was orating, as we heretofore stated.
That sum of all villainies—unclassified crime—
Started train of events bound to last thro' all time.
Like curst apple-eating through brave, eager Eve,
Whom serpent, by God damned, didst meanly deceive,
That rent in light trousers turned tide in affairs—
Threw more than one headlong down politics' stairs.
But murder will out; so at last didst attack
Bold miscreant made behind Jersey lad's back.
Good merchant, persistent, at last by slight bribe
(E'en men in New Jersey may be reached on that side),
Discovered damned culprit, of whom we'll dispose
Just partially here ere this canto we close.
Deep villain was young; also of those fellows
Whom citizens said would end on shame's gallows;

He didn't end so, but very many contended
That that death, at least, at last should him ended;
But we as reporter, true telling this tale,
Here give but his name, which some partisans hail.
Then let it be known—well remembered by all—
That seat was assailed—that lad made to fall,
In small town in New Jersey, where crime's discuss'd still—
Lad's seat was assailed by David B. Hill!
Behold well base caitiff! Cold, resolute eye
Knave far worse than Judas, Burr, Benedict—spy!
Fair freedom's outrager! Base, Satan-sent fiend
To strangle each right patriot blood, men, redeemed!
Plutocracy's idol? Damned dastard who'd drag
Through filth—rend forever—our fathers' proud flag!
Mark well—remember! In mind keep—in sight—
For, men, he Nemesised foully Fat Knight.
But, thank God Almighty, at last Knight so brave
In glory triumphed o'er keen, cursed knave,
Knight's deed last terrestrial.

THE FAT KNIGHT

TRAVELS, ACHIEVEMENTS, AMBITION.

Bold youth's departure; sibyl sent;
Dream, fortune, fate—just what each meant.
Steve's rapid rise; how he, when fossil
Practical, bulged out colossal.
Scup captured, lost; Knight paws up earth;
Sage manifesto with strange birth.

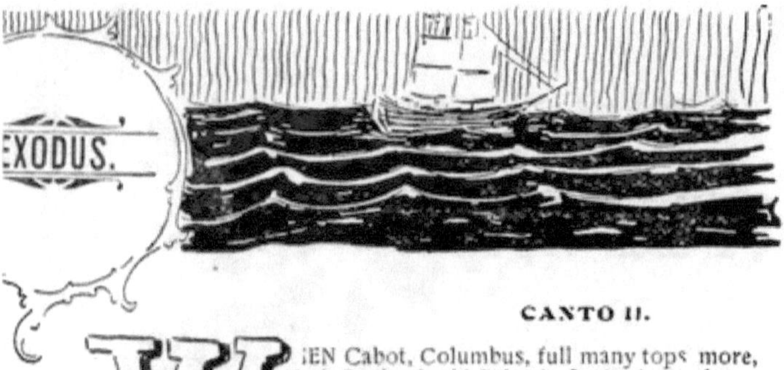

CANTO II.

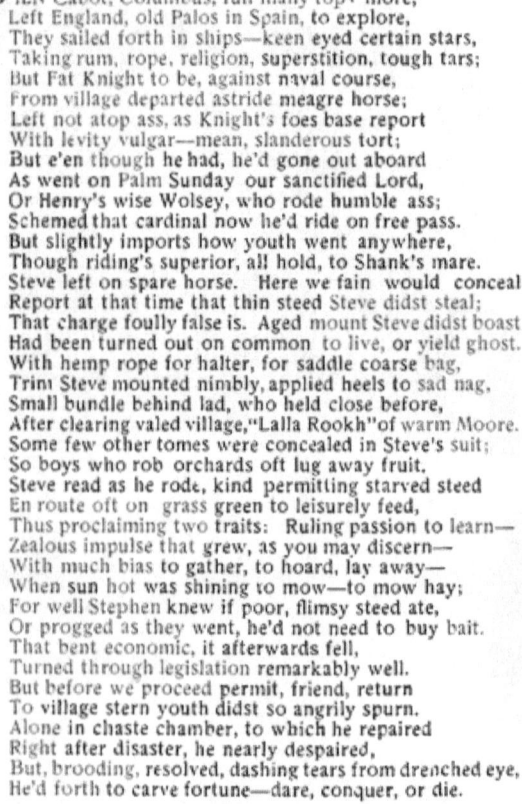

WHEN Cabot, Columbus, full many tops more,
Left England, old Palos in Spain, to explore,
They sailed forth in ships—keen eyed certain stars,
Taking rum, rope, religion, superstition, tough tars;
But Fat Knight to be, against naval course,
From village departed astride meagre horse;
Left not atop ass, as Knight's foes base report
With levity vulgar—mean, slanderous tort;
But e'en though he had, he'd gone out aboard
As went on Palm Sunday our sanctified Lord,
Or Henry's wise Wolsey, who rode humble ass;
Schemed that cardinal now he'd ride on free pass.
But slightly imports how youth went anywhere,
Though riding's superior, all hold, to Shank's mare.
Steve left on spare horse. Here we fain would conceal
Report at that time that thin steed Steve didst steal;
That charge foully false is. Aged mount Steve didst boast
Had been turned out on common to live, or yield ghost.
With hemp rope for halter, for saddle coarse bag,
Trim Steve mounted nimbly, applied heels to sad nag,
Small bundle behind lad, who held close before,
After clearing valed village, "Lalla Rookh" of warm Moore.
Some few other tomes were concealed in Steve's suit;
So boys who rob orchards oft lug away fruit.
Steve read as he rode, kind permitting starved steed
En route oft on grass green to leisurely feed,
Thus proclaiming two traits: Ruling passion to learn—
Zealous impulse that grew, as you may discern—
With much bias to gather, to hoard, lay away—
When sun hot was shining to mow—to mow hay;
For well Stephen knew if poor, flimsy steed ate,
Or progged as they went, he'd not need to buy bait.
That bent economic, it afterwards fell,
Turned through legislation remarkably well.
But before we proceed permit, friend, return
To village stern youth didst so angrily spurn.
Alone in chaste chamber, to which he repaired
Right after disaster, he nearly despaired,
But, brooding, resolved, dashing tears from drenched eye,
He'd forth to carve fortune—dare, conquer, or die.

Though young, Steve was manly; so, fixing plain clothes,
Precise packing up, sought his bed—sweet repose.
He dreamed when deep slumbered. Like Jacob of old
Didst vision—delusion delightful—behold.
Steve saw not long ladder, but drempt he held fast,
Controlled with his wisdom, holding firm in vice grasp,
Auric yield, silver shining, coal, commerce, trade,
High tariff, all shipping, Hawaii, whilst made
Great senates, hoar houses, old, proud party kneel,
From his lips taking law, nor dared to appeal.
He dreamed he reflected pure light of all suns;
He dreamed in high wisdom he weighed many tons;
He dreamed his importance invested all earth;
He dreamed none surpassed him in foresight, true worth;
He dreamed he was Jackson—Tom Jefferson, too;
He dreamed how he myriads of waterfowl slew;
He dreamed he as ruler would cut ripest cheese;
He dreamed he as pres'dent himself alone'd please;
He dreamed how in Wall street they'd give him applause;
He dreamed he'd suggest—make all nations' laws;
He dreamed he'd make merry, but not be scoff's sot;
He dreamed Uncle Sam should provide him stanch yacht;
He dreamed he'd expand—he'd become mighty hearty;
He dreamed himself better than any damned party;
He dreamed he was Cæsar, of whom lad had heard;
He dreamed he was eagle, proud national bird;
He dreamed he was Luther at diet of Worms;
He dreamed with old England he'd be on good terms;
He dreamed of Napoleon, most marvelous man;
He dreamed as tried statesman he stood in fame's van;
He dreamed he was Crœsus, who wallowed in gold;
He dreamed his renown high was billion years old;
He dreamed he was George, who cut cherry tree;
He dreamed he was led by most high destiny;
He dreamed he was Moses whom God telegraphed;
He dreamed he was Webster—Dan's noble shade laughed;
He dreamed when he snuffed all Bourbons should sneeze;
He dreamed when he'd nod all should drop on their knees;
He dreamed that as poet he surpassed supreme Bill;
He dreamed economic he'd eclipse even Mill;

Lola

He dreamed he was cutting as e'er Moliere;
He dreamed he was trenchant e'en more than Voltaire;
He dreamed every Mugwump rare sum of all worth;
He dreamed he, like Atlas, held up solid earth;
He dreamed he alone was all there's in space;
He dreamed Charles A. Dana base fraud, stain, disgrace;
He dreamed he was born to save ebon queen;
He dreamed he was Hagenbeck's menagerie team;
He dreamed he was chaster than ice, virtue, snow;
He dreamed he'd surpass in speech Cicero;
He dreamed he was Lola Montes, Nellie Gwynn;
He dreamed he could never commit mortal sin;
He dreamed he'd hang Irish remarkably well;
He dreamed in his day he'd raise political hell;
He dreamed he with Gresham would dove-tail with ease;
He dreamed he, like Neptune, 'd be god of all seas;
He dreamed of tobacco, cigars, snuff, cheroot;
He dreamed it heroic to supply substitute;
He dreamed of mud catfish full English mile high;
He dreamed he saw ducks in squads waddle by;
He dreamed silver free for worse than Cain's crime;
He dreamed civil service he'd repair in due time;
He dreamed in sound there is more than in sense;
He dreamed party pledges are of small consequence;
He dreamed of genius who answered to Hoke;
He dreamed every platform at best's merest joke;
He dreamed avid East deserved very best;
He dreamed raucous asses are South, immense West;
He dreamed chilly North then perhaps well enough;
He dreamed burly Bissell fit, fat, candent stuff;
He dreamed golden bonds were Sam's true golden mean;
He dreamed he could never know female unclean;
He dreamed bland bond broker just beyond all compare;
He dreamed monometal God's catholicon rare; [song;
He dreamed he would chant for chaste Mugwump sweet
He dreamed he could never be possibly wrong;
He dreamed high new standard of right he'd proclaim;
He dreamed will of party he'd indorse, then disdain;
He dreamed time would come to behold him boom'd boss;
He dreamed he'd be worshiped like Chinaman's joss;
He dreamed he would prove great men may be dull;
He dreamed certain men may be "splendidly null;"

Nell

He dreamed how dull ass by chance strange may rule;
He dreamed with false platform men people may fool;
He dreamed prudent star seeks inferior support;
He dreamed cabinets should e'er be chief's sport;
He dreamed men are great by being compared;
He dreamed for rich East very worst should be dared;
He dreamed he was idol of unalloyed gold;
He dreamed it all right if dull chief nation sold;
He dreamed "desuetude" very wonderful word;
He dreamed "innocuous" just simply superb;
He dreamed greatest statesman is principally beef;
He dreamed Hick'ry Bourbon far worse than sneak thief;
He dreamed he was sent by plain order from God;
He dreamed all bog Irish were ordained to tote hod;
He dreamed he was Alfred—King Frederick so great;
He dreamed he was king who said "I am state;"
He dreamed he was Swift, who grew glum—so flighty;
He dreamed he was Jesus, Holy Ghost, God Almighty;
He dreamed of Gudger, Botts, Slupsky, Pod, Hoke;
He dreamed till day's dawning, then Steve "wide awoke."
Arising, quick dressing, brief breathing pure prayer,
Collecting effects, sneaking shyly down stair,
He beheld that fine prospect—fair morning serene
Slow stealing forth softly, unfolding calm scene
Enchanting. In azure clear away off—afar
In lateral concave—sole stood silver star
Day's monarch to welcome, then pale disappear
To watch flaming rajah's fixed, regal career,
Peering star through blue shrinking; so oft children shy
Peep thro' prickly hedge when proud splendor sweeps by.
Limpid dawn lavished beauty. Rank grass white with dew
Bent 'neath lustral load; fairy flowers bowed, too,
Still seeming to slumber, excepting some bold—
Tall, alert hollyhock, sunflower with gold.
New Jersey is vapid, but can on occasion
Put up dewy morn in beauty amazing,
Like her melons mellic, which often we see go
Through thick lips to heart of glad, indolent negro.
So, too, her prime peaches, for which natives charge you
As if peaches reared down in old, glorious Georgia.
Glad sun, sombre lad, arising together,
Essayed day eventful with very fine weather—

Fresh air filled with balm, which lad filled his chest with,
Then started ahead fated fortune to wrest with,
Remarking en route, tho' then stripling tender,
That singular softness—pearl, calm, pensive splendor—
Investing dark woods, fragrant meadows, gray hills,
Vined village, lush gardens, green sward skirting rills
That gossiped along among stones, sturdy weeds,
As clear water rattled away to tall reeds
That never word uttered, but stood stiff, proudly stark,
Like aristocrats oft who deign no remark.
But leaves whispered kindly when lad passed along;
Birds joyous more sweetness poured into each song;
Sweet flowers, who'd watched him with love every day,
Were silvered with tears as he went sad away.
All faultless, too, envied bloom festal he chose
To cull from curved stem—fond caress with pleased nose.
Large, croconic blossom; 'twas not, as churls hold,
Meek cowslip, some cultured call marsh marigold.
By taking up xanthic when ruby, white, blue,
With other dyed flowers, abounded, he threw
Cold water full into face flaccid we've seen—
Old Galen's; Gal said lad would prize argentine.
But that's not important when there are so few
Who, when foretelling, sibylline what is true.
Your prophets are humbugs—mere loud-sounding brass;
E'en those called inspired are scarce fit to pass.
With large flavous rose, few effects, hope, remorse,
Cheese, crackers, bag, books, Steve sees feeble horse.
Lad made for thin charger, thin steed turned to him—
Both outcasts alike, so lad thought, madid, dim
Winsome eyes dry till then. Poor youth had true heart
Then soft as young mother's, now like vitreous dart.
So remorseless hard world is, so cruel, so cold,
'Tis odd any heart still is tender when old.
But old horse looked warm welcome; he seemed to regret
Sea saline boy shed, crystal flood, when they met
There early sheen morning. Frail horse had had woes,
Grand triumphs, disasters, caresses, scars, blows;
There sorely remembered what plaudits he wrung
From want, beauty, wealth, pride, as racer when young;
How lustrous large eye! How noble neck proud!
How away like wild wind! How huzzaed calid crowd!

How fair ladies adored him! How loveliest maid.
Her soft arms 'round arched neck, rose, roric lips, laid
To his velvet muzzle, gave him fervid kiss!
Ah, thought friendless horse, what unkind world is this!
Though liking lad's looks, clever, worldly-wise horse
Smelt his hands, garments, feet—big, lush rose, of course;
Then submitted to harness—rope halter, coarse bag—
Poor trappings that really amused skinny nag,
He showing much mirth by shaking ridged side
With borborygmal cachinnation. With pride
Bony crowbait, when lad firm sat on sharp back,
Essayed to perform as of yore on fast track,
Which Steve soon discouraged, for through fabric thin
Backbone of Buceph galled sorely lad's skin
Which smarted, sharp, biting, saliferous sweat—
Nag's side a l in lather, lad's legs with it wet—
Eating into red chafes, inflicting keen pain;
So lad wise, steed halting, dismounting, took rein;
Trim legs wide apart, Steve walked slow before
Kind friend who, unwitting, had made Steve so sore.
Thus mile or so trudged; then, refreshed by stiff breeze,
Camped under smooth beech, in which, on his knees,
Steve name deeply carved, with date, with week day;
Art work you may see if you happen that way.
Whilst carving intently, thought mirrored in face,
Approached lad chief sibyl of scattered, swart race
Native by Indus. When their eyes met sweet smile
Illumined strange face. No shade there of guile
Accredited tribes who suggest fabled Jew
Fated restless to wander through earth, as in Sue,
But truth, trust, devotion, fidelity, cheer.
"I come, boy," sonorous sound charms artist's ear;
"I come, boy, at last! In bright vales whence I come—
Oh, beauteous world! Pungul, Udipur, Sum!
Bengal, Sumatra, Bap, Mandalay, Siam!
Calcutta, Tumkar, Tonk, Ganges, Jheend, Assam!
From Kundus to Kotar—Kuntcote to Bangkok—
Of thee legends live—of thee doth each man talk—
Hosts, too, sung for ages! Seers, too, have predicted
Thy birth, rise, high station. Me, once interdicted,
Picked they earth to round lest something dark, tragic
Arrested thy progress by threatening Scup Magic.

Siam's Crown Prince

My people are wise in all mystical lore;
In dreams, signs, traditions. Long, long time before
Thy birth they knew thee. I come from far coast
To tell thee what told them once India ghost.
He said in New Jersey one time wouldst arise
Brave babe who as Knight wouldst all earth surprise.
He said babe at birth wouldst incline to bright moon;
Wouldst point to pale night queen; that little gossoon
Wouldst bear ruddy mark upon smooth, snowy part;
Wouldst much learning absorb; vast wisdom impart
Whilst yet in cradle. Ghost so sage said also
That singular babe wouldst have truculent foe
Who wouldst base seek to steal, to gratify hate,
Rare fish, Magic Scup, babe with hook, line, live bait,
Wouldst catch when man grown. Magic Scup, said grave
seer,
Babe, youth, man, or Knight, shouldst prize very dear,
For if preserved it wouldst raise holder higher
Than any before dared to even aspire.
So here, son, I warn thee! Be thou on thy guard!
Preserve well thy Scup! I have said."
Fond regard
Dark sibyl paid youth as slow, backing, withdrew,
Seeming almost to fade, like fog when pierced through
Sun's gold, gorgeous bars. Awhile pensive sat Steve;
Then carving resumed; little told could believe,
But many years after, though gay, sober, tipsy,
Oft thought he with awe of dark, Indus gypsy.

Rude carving completed, hunger lad to appease
Assailed crackers, onions, cucumbers, rice, cheese:
Oryza in pudding coy maid back in village
Secured for loved lad, for whom she didst pillage,
Plunder, sack, ravage—swift go through fat larder,
She inspired by pity, but love lending ardor.
As he ate he beheld her. Great tears to each eye
Welling up in hot flood tumbled down on plum pie
So deep, ample, juicy. Such some women make
On farms in Ohio—in perhaps other state,
But never in city. There baker rogues know
Cash value of filling—of each ounce of dough—
Never more putting in, never more putting 'round,
Than laws stern command. Ample lunch on spiced ground
Put Stephen to thinking. He remembered he'd read,
But couldn't tell where, traveled author had said

Men who pyr'mids erected had lived upon rice.
Cucumbers, leeks, onions; yellow John messed on mice;
Monmouth ate peas green; fine French feast on frogs,
Whilst redskins regale with great gusto on dogs.
Lo, lazy vag sannup! Grave, noble, red man
Who smells rye in fleet wind! So longs for filled can!
Who stinks in coarse blanket, eats mule, defies law,
Is pest ward of nation—dirty curse of swart squaw;
Proof inscrutable Lord unwisely may reign,
At times for some reason performing part vain.
We said lad beheld maid. He did so in truth.
In all her fat beauty, frank goodness, sweet youth,
But not in fair person. She sat sensate queen
On throne of his heart—ruled she there blessed, supreme;
There fond he beheld her. Dropping now on his knee
He paid her warm homage—her slave swore he'd be
For life—aye, forever. He vowed he would love her;
Youth's full of such flame, which often breeds bother.
Keen hunger appeased, with soft arm 'neath fair cheek,
Upon fragrant sod soon snored he in sleep.
He slept very sound; then most marvelous thing,
Surpassing Jules Verne, sagas weird Norsemen sing,
Surprised shadow steed, blithe birds, rufous cow,
Who saw awful wonder, unrevealed until now.
We give news exclusive, so think we may whoop,
Indulging self-praise, because of clean scoop,
Pursuing broad path Magyar Pulitzer treads
When World sneaks defile men, if not marriage beds,
As doth McLean's sheets, some others, each spewer
Of foul filth offending from festering sewer.
As youth sweetly slumbered, firm mouth open wide,
With flies buzzing 'round, 'mazed exploring inside
That seemed to bold insects miraculous cave,
Thro' earth's vast, granite heart passed tremulous wave
Like one late 'neath Florence. Scared youth, rock'd awake,
Endeavored to stand, but could not for earth's quake.
He reeled, staggered, wavered; he acted like vag
Uncertainly steering large, picturesque jag.
Whilst earth worked in tremor, was convulsed so within;
Mad storm raged without. Like tumult ne'er 'd been,
So all oldest cits said, in Jersey before;
Hail, wind, lightning, thunder, rain, darkness, deep roar,

Made grand, dreadful conflict—some shrinking souls pray
Good, great God Almighty fierce storm's strife to stay.
E'en preachers so prayed, preferring, it seemed,
To stay on earth rather than above pure, redeemed.
Whilst priest, preacher, pope, declare all in deep woe,
Sin-stained,curst, wretched,all earth worthless show,
They cling to low life with grip quite as tenacious
As wretches abandoned, men most contumacious.
Staid cloth's inconsistent, yet proper grave cloth
As smooth factor social; wise men are not wroth
With fat, hearty fellows who Scripture expound,
Pullet tender preferring to mutton, flitch, round.
They're handy at weddings; one time, too, were known
Fit mates for meek maidens mere trifle fly-blown,
As find in Macaulay, who's rare discourse on
Sound preaching,gay wedding, of scorned English parson.
But mortal with Bible on end of trained tongue
Has ever apt answer though he herd among
Professors, grave judges, wise senators even,
So grand is good book God gave us from heaven,
Or didn't, as Ingersoll ever maintains—
Blithe colonel who mixes eld truth with bright brains;
He says little new, but silver, pure gold,
He gives us from quartz from rich mines very old.
Bob may go to hell, but if he to hot lake
Is condemned, it is certain God'll make once mistake,
For Bob with kind creed, surpassing Jerome,
Would adorn highest heaven—yea, porphyry throne.
But if Bob go to glory, how many popes there,
Jack Wesley, Mart Luther, Black, Wycliffe, wilt stare!
For likely they all hope to see Bobby's ghost
Red devil most gleefully, totally toast,
More thoroughly scorching than ever in Spain
Flames holy of see burnt again, yet again;
Or fagots of Mary, whose most Christian food
Wast bishop quite crisp with hot, red human blood
As shed by Queen Bess, who swore hard,which was wrong;
Whose nose, like her reign, too, was rather too long.
But if Bob go to heaven, stern Calvin, hard Knox,
Wilt pray God Almighty to set up stiff stocks;
Torquemada, if there, wilt howl in Christ's name
For rack, inquisition, boots, thumb-screws, hell flame;

All merciful Medici, with good Borgia crew,
Wilt pray to see Bobby in lead molten stew;
If prayers are unheeded, whole, kind Cath'lic pack
May rise in revolt, God's heaven high sack,
They valorous murdering, like fiends shedding flood,
Bartholomew's kill, of Huguenot blood,
So pleasing pope perfect he ordered high mass,
Or vespers, Te Deum, or sainted some ass.
But we are straying from Stephen. Astagger, all pale,
He sorely was pelted by wind, rain, jagged hail;
There sure had he perished had not he been whirled
In funnel-shaped wind far above smitten world.
Mad whirl picked him up, as also thin horse,
Wild wafting lad on him with dread, fearful force
Up high in air amb'ent, him hurling on steed
Upward, mad onward, with incredible speed,
Gaunt horse always under, pale lad as if glued
To steed digging out as if all hell hot pursued.
Compared with their flight, wild dash of O'Shanter
Were merely brisk walk, slow jog, lazy canter,
Whilst Sheridan's ride—well, Phil's famous race
Is not to be thought of with Steve's frantic chase.
As they wildly flew up they also flew 'round,
Steve yelling, horse neighing, but ne'er slightest sound
Reached earth retreating, so terrifical roar
Affrighting New Jersey as mad hurricane tore
Destroying young crops, fell wrecking with ravage
Like unrestrained troops, or damned, painted savage.
Storm dug potatoes, tossed houses, fell fruit trees,
Killed swine, cattle, horses, some millions of hived bees;
Leveled fine woods down; left not taper steeple,
But, for great wonder, escaped all good people.
Wide view from above, where Stephen on steed
Wast sailing around, wast sublime, grand, indeed,
But neither took time, nor had inclination,
To note reckless grandeur investing creation,
But, with single purpose, one aim, settled thought,
At task then in hand persistently wrought.
We said task in hand, but to speak with more care
Twain's task then in hand was sore task much in air.
As upward they flew, neither lad nor lean horse
Attended one moment to determine true course,

But simply sped in disorder, fear, sorrow,
With never notion of map, route, to-morrow;
They stuck to their job; sore they moiled as if mad—
As if other labor were not to be had—
Unmindful of boycott, close union, vain strike,
Reduction of hours, more pay, or such like,
Hopes so often engaging men now who unite
Hard logic of trade, truth of Mill, too, to fight,
As if ever union, or socialist band,
Could defy, could defeat, supply—store—demand,
Which invincible rule—as sternly control
As moons, blazing suns, or loadstones at North pole.
Debs, Powderly, Irons, McBride, all their kind,
Are misled, or knavish, or totally blind.
Men who toil are but stock, like coke, coal, or ore,
Grain, lumber, fat cattle, or goods kept in store;
Each toiler's cheap unit whose value is high
Or low in accordance with market supply.
That's all there is in it despite noisy Lease
With demagogues like her who disturb public peace.
Harp, scribble, howl, thunder, by night, by fair day,
For so much coin per hour. To Botany Bay
Transport paltry pack! Men are sick of slush, lingo,
Lies, twaddle, poppycock, they issue, by jingo!
Simpson, Waite, Peffer, all their likes with loose jaw,
Would enrich all on earth by process of law;
By "Be it enacted" in senate, lodge, house,
Goulds make of all those now as poor as church mouse;
Through law, not through labor, from all want release us,
Thus making each toiler proud Vanderbilt Crœsus,
Having cash so abundant it wouldn't be worth
As much as Pop speeches, or farmed-to-death earth;
Coin cabbage, flax, hay, shucks, cordwood; mint hoop-
poles—
Make dollars of doughnuts, Pop wind into pistoles!
Let Peffers prevail; Kansas Simpsons control;
At head of great nation put Populist mole;
Turn schools into caucus; wild politics preach
From pulpits where Jesus now few deign to teach;
Disdain proven custom; call work crowning crime—
Salt sweat rankest stigma; out of joint swear is time;
Damn all men in power; all rich declare knaves;
Call capital tyrant; men poor cry are slaves;

Sockless Sage Simpson

So loudly proclaim, whilst, for peroration,
By-God straight to hell is rushing this nation.
With platform so terse, propositions so plain,
Join Peffer, Debs, Altgeld, making cogent campaign.
Never urge men to labor; your lips never soil
Declaring how conquest attends ever toil;
Ne'er say true to youth: Each boy's best assistant
Is not tutor stern, but Mr. Persistent;
Stick, then you'll succeed; work, strive, hard persist;
Resolve firm to win, then you must; how long list
Of names great in science, law, letters, war, art,
Were shortened if each had not had stoutest heart!
Fame walks not on roses, but mostly long road
Is steep, rugged, broken; quite frequent sore load
Like lead weights down pilgrim, but resolute will
At last reaches summit of mountain, high hill;
Rests, then, on tiptop, looking back o'er long way
With proud exultation that won is fight—day;
But teach women, men, all youth, even babies,
That they to succeed must contract Peffer rab'es.
But is this not digression? Is't fair to thin steed,
To Steve, or keen critics, thus loose to proceed?
Can we hope for sweet puff with such slips, sins, delays—
Anticipate even cold curse of "faint praise"?
Offending so vicious—disdaining set rules
Held sacred so long by revered, wisest schools—
May we not have occasion to think with deep curse
Of damnable day that seduced us to verse?
Be that as it may—be all this counterfeit—
There now is no help—what is written is writ,
Nor change single word, single thought, single verse,
But on with this epic for better, or worse,
Not e'en consenting to believe it fault, blur,
When rhymes quite alike very frequent recur.

Elihu Burritt, the Learned Blacksmith.

Rising hero, thin horse, when we looked at them last,
Were making for heaven remarkably fast;
We greatly regret rigid truth makes us own
Pure pair never reached God's golden, grand throne.
Very high they ascended, but never so high
As to be out of view from terrestrial eye,
Which saw them in awe, beheld them with wonder,
As onward they hurtled midst hail, rain, dread thunder.

In fierce funnel-shaped wind, in which, now less wild,
Quite remarkable thing didst remarkable child.
Aeronautics, exciting, keen whetted lad's hunger—
You know how we ate when we all were younger.
He, though in great peril, reached into chuck sack
Wind god fetched along; from store took ample snack,
Which coolly he ate as they sailed through wild sky—
Food, we must confess, was just plain apple pie—
Most manifest proof of Steve's nerve. Could you eat
Awhirl high in murk air had you sat in Steve's seat?
Could Cæsar so? Could Lee, Grant, or Hannibal,
Been so intrepid on ascending animal?
Could Napoleon so dined, or Frederick, called great,
Ever had eaten were he so situate?
Could mute Miles, or Scofield, asail at such height,
Had soul, or stout stomach, to talk, eat, or fight?
We stay not to answer—to argue—but state
Not one ever did. Upward, on at great rate
Proceeded pair madly as if wanted soon,
Or expected, awaited, to dine at high noon.
As lad rode he reflected. Farther up he from land
Much more, so it seemed, his young soul didst expand.
He had widest view, which pensive bard tells us
From narrow deductions in time repels us.
Or cramped soul doth widen; so, also, great sorrow
Oft's good for proud rich, sin-stained, chilly narrow.
Lad thought of old dicta, of which very few,
Though sounding superb, are in fact wholly true,
As sage saw about hills, declared ever green
If off afar elevations are seen.
An utter untruth! Purple, hazy, or gray,
Is hill high, or mountain, we see far away,
Or some mystic shade, but ne'er parraceous hue
Of Irishman's shamrock—oft wild Irishman, too.
Another false adage dogmatic declares
Man cannot excel in fine art, or affairs,
Without labor great, when it's patent truth still
Supreme talent only complete filleth bill.
Where's excellent art where talent is not?
Slow work of hard striving stands mostly but rot.
True, all masters study, but all were in vain
Were they not equipped with magnificent brain.

No excellence is where talent with fire,
Or genius, is lacking, no odds what desire.
Stolid ass may essay to sing serenade,
But he'll nothing but bray, though papers parade
He studied with Patti, in Rome, or fair Paris,
Where's Bernhardt bewitching, with much that so rare is.
No excellence is without there's great labor
Is false as firm fact, kind reader, or neighbor,
But all must admit in one way is quite true—
To plodders applying—to all but rare few.
So thought our hero with much more in same strain
As onward he whirled in wind, hail, thunder, rain.
He tho't when you reason you're right say you're wrong;
Then improve, refine, polish, your speech, drama, song,
Your painting, or aught your parts strive to do,
Though composing mass major, or cobbling coarse shoe.
Remember that little superb must surpass
Loose raft careless done, or immense faulty mass.
He thought of small Welshmen, some English, bog Mick,
Who appear as if made by God to wield pick;
How sad, too, ambition so often is wedded
To men who can't soar because so thick-headed—
Men who long, dream, attempt, hard struggle, yet fail!
Christ, what cruel fate! Better kine in calm vale
Sweet, green meadow cropping, or swine whose pursuit
Is to grunt, gorge slops tainted, contentedly root.
For contentment is best. Ragged pauper with it,
Though he have nothing else, is affluent cit.
Golden chalice of care from which Cæsars sup
Is sad by smooth gourd, or brown cocoanut cup,
Contentment, though poorest, holds eager to lips,
Joy, peace, drinking down in sweet draughts, not in sips.
He thought asses all, if not voice-formed to bray,
Wouldst whistle incessant, if not surpliced to pray,
For praying, coarse braying—to say it's not treason—
Most perfectly rhyme—are much like in reason.
Good in orison found men plain may decry
In skeptical shot, "Pray, but power keep dry!"
Prayer had perfect test when sad nation implored—
On its knees begged blessed Virgin, Christ Jesus, God Lord,
That pres'dent to save who sunk by loved sea
Into unending sleep, deep revered by all free,

Sara.

His rest by old Erie, which in sunshine, dawn, gloom,
Grave calm, solemn tempest, guards faithful mourned
tomb—
Broods sent'nel with night, stands sent'nel with day,
To watch sacred spot where moulds cherished clay.
As lad sailed along he also gave thought
To contemptible men mean enough to be bought;
How small scurvy rascal, how cheap vulgar type,
Descending to entertain pistareen spite!
How common that person who can be content
Sneer, slight, or cold shoulder, to open resent!
What low cur bad temper! How weak, trying, mean,
Those men who habitually spit out puisne spleen!
For which, as live organ, no use has been named
Since Adam, sneak, coward, bonny bride basely blamed.
Away with churl cynic—continual kicker!
E'er greater plague than chump constant in liquor.
Vain, bitter fault-finder with spleen, rancor, ire,
At best 's but annoying, flat, fussy pismire.
He seldom is fat, whilst his eyes, logic, beak,
To accord with coarse brain, are habitually weak;
His eyes perhaps green, like late Marrowfat pea;
His nose glaucous, sharp, like great shark's in salt sea;
With more bowels than brains, though former are small,
Tart cynic's vain curse to himself—yea, to all
Compelled, or condemned, by hard, cruel fate,
To speak him, or hear him borborygmal berate.
But castigate not severely weak, mad ass,
For none other leads wretched life quite as sad as
Dark, bitter, hateful, chill, fretful, damned, dismal
One of crabbed cynic, whose life's hell abysmal,
Like that of poor fools who treasure up spite,
Appearing in spats, in tongue tilts, to delight.
From such, God, defend us! Too, keep away, Gcd,
Detestable jackass—pah! pest, cursed clod—
Gossip loquacious, who hankers to handle
Squabbles, tea-tempests, dogfights, lowest scandal,
He often repeating foul stuff stupid o'er—
Good God Almighty, why'd You make such fool bore?
But let us thank God since so kindly He hung
In Fat Knight comparative taciturn tongue.
He talked with apt purpose. When needed sound word,
Set speech, or wise order, voice valiant world heard.

But he more seldom said, except terse discourse
When he fished, roamed for duck, spur-urged saddle horse;
Then, with boom companions, at times when they'd
pottle,
He'd say, "Gimme bait," or "Pass me black bottle;"
But most of Knight's time, e'en when eating, deep drinking,
Mute fishing, sound sleeping, was devoted to thinking.
Ofttimes when he slept mind superb would revolve
Vast, grave, weighty problems—them readily solve.
'Tis said he thus drafted, surveying all facts,
Remarkable law for imposing stiff tax
Upon certain incomes. 'Twas never Knight's fault
Law declared highest court not worth pinch of salt;
Not all that court made he, so could urge demurrur
If charged with high crime when court made crude error.
Lad thought of quick living; he pondered dumb dead;
He soliloquized some, when substantially said:
Mere life is scarce shadow. To live—to slave, sleep—
With never ambition, were obloquy deep.
Attempt to excel. In each art—enterprise—
Not only do well, but perform to surprise.
Resolve to surpass. With rectitude, zest,
Hope, confidence, faith, do your positive best,
Remembering ever, as you strive to prevail here,
Slack, faint resolution's fertile father of failure.
Lad thought of village; of mishap with barrel;
Of Yank foe; of steed, whose color was sorrel;
Heart's idol—fat, fair maid; deep, juicy plum pie;
He thought he was sailing tremendously high,
Ne'er dreaming fierce flight so high up plain typic
Of what he'd carve out in career high politic.
But storm much abating—almost at an end—
Pelted pair slowly, easy, commenced to descend;
That is, slow compared with infernalest flight
When upward they flew, going nigh out of sight.
They landed at last, falling safe, light as cork,
On deck of Teutonic, White Star, for New York.
There was much consternation some time, mates, aboard,
Some sailors declaring lad with steed from dread Lord
Had fallen plumb, straight down; so too didst report
When tars, after landing, paid drunk, carnal court
To wenches grades lower than bawds pious paid
Before Parkhurst's agents to naked parade.

Though young yet our hero, his mind was ripe man's;
Stood tall as when tallest; his feet, ears, hams, hands,
Were nearly full-grown; but when stouter, older,
Big belly bulged out—grew greatly bolder.
Although of famed family much given to preach,
Fine youth in fair city soon started to teach
Pupils blind yet content, his intellect feeding
On study severe, scup, tautog, good reading.

The New Woman.
From Harper's Bazar.

He dipped into Byron; dipped, dived into Moore,
Each loving intense; cynic "Corsair" read o'er
To certain kind ladies, but never new woman,
Who never can match sweetest, matchless true woman.
But longed for far West; much longing, he started;
For Cleveland he packed; straightway, too, departed.
In Buffalo landing, prized plan he forsook,
Ripe scholarship lending to edit herd book

Kind relative issued. In it were in full
Long pedigrees perfect of cow, calf, heifer, bull,
Full many of which their great worth among men
Owe yet to our hero, who with busy pen
Depicted blood bovine, all fine points—reared tree
Of descent, giving true, chaste, full pedigree,
In which high occupation biographers tell
Good Fat Knight to be didst greatly excel.
He earned such distinction bull breeders extolled
His worth as fine author as often proud told
Their triumphs with bullocks, steers, heifers, cows, calves,
At home to close neighbors, hands, stout better-halves.
Youth's fame was so great he was accepted as chief
On every nice problem relating to beef.
He oft was called in when young cow was confined.
Sore event much appealing to Stephen's heart, mind
Rich as rare in resources, which free he applied
With signal success, with much pardonab'e pride.
Were cow in great labor, rough hind for relief
Would be sent on fleet charger to fetch renowned chief,
Who'd dash off to farm, to field, or cow stable,
Eager to render all relief he was able.
Very rarely he failed. With skill, with sharp steel,
He, as apt accoucheur, had vast luck with veal;
Same luck, too, attended when long after he set
Skilled hand to selection of state cabinet,
Which spite oft belittled, which malice would joke,
Bekase of one Bissell, of another, high Hoke—
With mean, forged allusions to dark, Island queen
At one time deposed; disposed too much to learn,
So said Knight's traducers, upon Knight, also friends
Who aided his projects, loud applauded his ends.
Low wits welted Quinton with fib, fustian flat,
Declaring him merely Repub-Democrat,
E'en though cultured colonel—in splendid career
Arose in wrong war to be brave brigadier;
Sad fell at Atlanta, since when, so sneer's scoff is,
He always had held, or been running for, office,

Vogue pair of professions now nearly all men,
Whilst hotly pursuing, most caustic condemn.
Office-seeker when out is sure it's shame, sin,
Place public to hold, but saint-like when he's in.
E'en Chauncey Depew, who gave prime, Punic spread
That political peace might hover o'erhead,
Like thin, thoughtful Ingalls, bold Sunflower pride,
Holds partisan paard paying, safest to ride.
'Tis probably so, for sleek, partisan steed
Is ever well-groomed, has abundant, fine feed,
Rich rubbers distinguished, is trained to trot through
Roads crooked, steep, rocky, ne'er casting calk shoe;
Yet occasion'ly falls, like Horace, false Reid,
Firm former apostate from Abe with just creed,
Whilst Whitelaw so feeble, so impotent, frail,
Defeated head potent whilst wagging weak tail.
But we stray from set purpose when we should pursue
Straight highway buff stretching ahead far in view;
Would, too, but green meadows, mute Edens, clear rills,
Vines, flowers, grain waving, creeks crooked, stern hills,
Alluring attract to stay, saunter, slow jog,
Noble nature surveying, sometimes from lone log;
Or, lazy reclining, through wondering eye,
Beneath frondent friend, ponder deep, profound sky
When cerulean sea, or black-clouded; or trace
Mystical monsters, magic wonders, in lace
Fair fringing vast concave, e'er taking on shapes
Now suggesting huge birds, now blue Alps, Afric apes;
Or watch in dim distance rude farmer afield,
Perhaps roundly cursing because court repealed
Lax law to tax incomes. Plow now, plodding slow,
Turns over sod fertile, dog's fennel lays low,
With tho'ts not directed 'gainst roots, rubbish, weeds,
But resolving political problems, planks, needs,
Whilst newspaper reading, study well in its way,
But too much indulged by light masses today.
Since journals are few caring, daring, to rise
Above party bias, peccant prejudice, lies,
Petty scandals, court dirt, cheap cuts, coarse abuse,
With little instructive, much less to amuse,

Sheets' influence nil despite proud, profuse boast
At banquet whenever "The Press" is trite toast.
There are editors true, but mostly are seen
Dirty waste used to wipe some master's machine
Per so much paid wipe. Some others incline
By printing spitz spite spurned foes to malign,
Whilst others, like Fox, with pink, pus Gazette,
McLean, Magyar, Dunlop, puke out rank poudrette—
Mere venders of filth—noted buzzards, hawks, crows,
Ouraging all sense, deep disgusting taste's nose;
Employers of sneaks far-famed to excel
Hound, cur, pointer, ratter, in matter of smell—
Reporters delighting in airing foul linen,
Damned, dirtiest deeds of loose men, depraved women;
Enjoying high art, or delectable trade,
Of journalist ostler, vile sheet's chambermaid,
Inhaling with unction, as if sweetest guerdon,
Smells, stenches, arising rank up from squat jordan—
Aye, holding them rarer than rose, apple, pink,
Red clover, swine, polecat—all other strong stink.
Social-sewer explorers! Tars eager to sail
To discover retreats of men lewd, women frail,
Looking into their lives, behind their back doors,
Into bedrooms, close closets, scab souls, chancres, sores—
Delighting in dirt—glad declaring most excellent
Everything fetid, foul, filthy, feculent;
But superior, by far, paid sneaks when deployed
To contrast, or compare, with whom they're employed,
As soon found our hero, who held in contempt
Tribe almost entire. Very few he'd exempt
From proclaimed bitter scorn, in which, to tell truth,
He showed keen discernment, but he was acute youth.
Though wielding paid pen he knew his plain prose,
His standing, were higher than record of those
Employed with goose quill on hebdomedal journal,
Tri-weekly, monthly, handbill, dull diurnal.
Though author himself he held it ill trade
Best writer, close reader, both apt to degrade,
His views on vexed subject quite pointed, clear, terse,
He giving one day, much as follows, in verse:

Books make us no better, but rather impair
Minds, morals of men, leading many from prayer.
How can we be pious when bad, sparkling tomes
So allure us in shops, on trains, in sweet homes?
How pure when most papers, abundant as leaves,
Print all foulness, facts filthy—how woman deceives,

Men riot, Thugs murder, wives sin, preachers fall—
Priests wanton, belles slip when champagned at swell
ball—
Give all scandal high with all nude scandal low;
Paint conduct disgusting of actor, bawd, beau;
Seductions, divorces, adulteries, rapes,
Incest, fornication—all Sotadic scrapes?
But there are exceptions: some books may be read
Reforming heart hardest, improving teak head;
But such works are rare, whilst much wider grows waste,
Vile, vicious supplanting true, clean, noble, chaste.
Though Steve's pen was purest, it depicting best breed
Of cattle, their families, past, future, fame, feed,
Steve fell in revolt, great alarmed lest his pen
Might tainted become—be infected by men
Employed on press venal; he clearly foresaw
Impending result, so embraced abstruse law,

Beginning with Blackstone. By night, by long day,
Sir William Steve studied, learning how to convey,
Of escheat, bail, enfeoff, torts, leases, entail,
Escrow, bond, escuage, sequester, deed, sale,
Glebe, socage, advowson, abaction, soforth,
Law then in this country of little or no worth.
He read up on murder, benefice, parish,
As well as best way to hang up wild Irish,
Which one time he did, adjusting stout halter
As if hangman born; without hitch, or fault, or
Puerile compunction, or trying delay, even,
He sent them to heaven, didst good Sheriff Stephen.
No better Jack Ketch e'er fixed firm fatal noose—
E'er cooked more artistic tough Irishman's goose;
No bungling, no horror, no mangling of muscle,
As when they did Monmouth, hacked noble Lord Russell,
But smooth as skilled skater skims over slick ice
Steve worked off pale pair, collected prized price;

Fair omen, again, he would certain arise
His name to adorn, waning world save, surprise,
As doctor predicted loquacious, fine night
Babe first seeing moon so admired her light.
Few hangmen grow great, but leaving grim gibbet
Our hero high talent didst forthwith exhibit.
Latent genius developed; he expanded so fast
Soon Calcraft, soon Marwood, our worthy surpassed,
Besides far outstripping, though lately mere child,
So noted immortal as Jonathan Wild.
Steve's fame filled his county; soon grew, too, so great
Full invested with wonder each inch of York state.
Pursuing coy law close by night as by day,
To bar gained admission in fair month of May
In year '59, year Brown fell at Ferry—
For slaves started battle. John, hanged in some hurry,
Mad war pushed along, which reached bloody crisis
When lusty Stephen held primitive office,
From which he was drafted, when bravely he borrowed,
Cash getting stout sub Steve valiant sent for'ard
Whilst like proven hero, at work as attorney,
He waged war in court—of Mars awful son he!
He battled for fees; fell, fiercely contended
With mouth, not with musket, as daily defended
State's side of cases, rightly holding grim war,
Right's highest trial, all just men should abhor,
Agreeing with Quakers, nuns, virgins, good wives,
How God, never men, should take away lives,
Revering commandments God flashed unto Moses,
Who himself slew his man, as Scripture discloses,
In sand corse concealing. 'Twas later in sewer
Na-Gael coffined Cronin, whose killing caused furore
Stamping base Clan with its tough Mcs, hellish O's,
Damnest villains, curs, cowards—infernalest foes
Befouling fair earth. Steve sticking to cases,
Wild bog-trotters hanging, correcting all races,
Waxed fat in finance, galore gathered gear,
His wage being even six hundred each year,
With vast store of learning from tenure to tariff,
High duties of bailiff, with province of sheriff,

Latter office accepting as well for rest, ease,
As executive practice with fairly fat fees,
With time to renew application to law,
Then revealing slight rust. Though young, Stephen saw,
As with eye of prophet, his country might call
On him to take charge along in some fall
To rule, great reform; so to hard study bent
Attention in office, tho' on duty intent.
Made sheriff in '70, in '74
He went back to practice as he had before.
But soon, fortune smiling, no goddess more fair,
Behold, bulky hero is Buffalo's mayor!
Two steps up long ladder soon after, then we
Behold nation's chief is famed Fat Knight to be,
When spread his true greatness—that splendid career
All men in this country, all nations, revere,
For Red Top he purchased with sundry more lots
Besides knitting to him Gott Dusty, Dome, Botts,
Topp, Slupsky, Pod Dismuke, Skaggs, Mugwumps, Queen
Lil,
Steve Brodie, Beecher, Jay Snigg, Harper's, Bill
Colonel News Brown, Artist Keppler, pert Puck;
Some said, too, Rome's pope. Goldbugs ran amuck
In Wall street with joy whilst Carl Schurz, Pound,
Blair,
With Codman, one Wadleigh, with huzzas filled murk air.
Full many cheered, staggered, but after four years,
According to papers, another appears
To fill highest place; then Knight went away
To Bangs, Stetson, Tracy, great Lawyer MacVeagh,
In Gotham remaining until '93,
When dawned as Fat Knight with majestic degree.
Though superb before, it is perfectly clear
He now far surpassed all his former career.
After Knight's second triumph colossal, with line,
Hooks, bait, bottles, cards, friends perhaps eight or nine,
Knight went forth to fish. Knight with jagged, jolly lot
Wild carnival held in trim vessel loaned—yacht.
They feasted, they lushed, they laughed, they played,
swore;
They told shady stories—did as most men before
Did on such occasions—will contine to do.
Men seldom had seen more jagged, reckless crew.

Brodie.

They'd but sat down to play without limit when
Declared beaming Knight, "Poker, boys, now and then
By best men is relished." Long, boisterous roar
Told how palpable hit Knight chanced thus to score.
Till after 3 playing at last they turned in,
Tumbling up, falling down, making damnable din.
Slept they all very late deep sleep of deep drunk,
Then arose they with heads on. Last from his bunk
Fat Knight appeared, nigh concealing hot head
Bag filled with cracked ice; eyes, nose, his face, red.
Some cocktails consuming, to breakfast repaired;
That eaten then all for day's fishing prepared.
With uncommon care Fat Knight looked to reel,
To bait, to long pole, to stout line, hooks of steel,
But showed no emotion, his inscrutable face
Disclosing no shadow of thought holding place
In soul discomposed much. That day had recurred
With full force to mind all from sibyl he'd heard;
Remembered prediction crone midwife had made;
Felt plain hand of fate then most heavily laid
On apex of heart. Through large frame crept cold chill
Close followed by fever, but resolute will
Concealed inward tumult. E'en each round of drinks
Impression made not, but calm, cold, stern as sphinx
Forth cast fated barb. In dark deep swallowed up
Grave moment, then bite, then strong pull, then, lo, Scup!
Knight observed magic sign; then fell he flat, prone
Extended on deck, nor word, nor sigh, groan,
From bloodless lips issued. Quick kneeling, close chum,
Feeling Knight's pulses, yelled frantic, "Fetch rum!"
They all gather'd 'round; they chafed him much, bathed;
Poured rye on his head; his neck thick, his hands
swathed;
Pounded, punched, pinched, him; unbuttoned his collar
To let him have air; tried to get "him to swaller,"
As one kind heart suggested. That remedy wise
Proved most efficacious. Knight opened wide eyes
Just after they poured, through pried-open mouth,
Full half quart of whisky. Knight looked to murk South;
Then East; then to North; then he looked to red West;
Then said he, "I'm faint. Lemme lay till I rest."

But they would not consent. They raised him instead,
That stout crew entire; they conveyed him to bed,
Where remained till next day, when found he his catch
In water alive. None had seen that Scup's match.
They had early observed those significant TT's
Near dorsal fin prickly. Knight, pointing, said: "These
Bear out prediction once made unto me
When lad sat I carving my name in beech tree
Near town in New Jersey. They vindicate, too,
Strange words of crone midwife when child once I knew,
What those two predicted it becomes me not now
To more fully explain. But wish you would vow
In case Scup is taken, or stolen, or lost,
It you'll help recover no odds how great cost."
Each gladly took vow, then serene sailed away,
As Knight would not hear of one moment's delay,
For city of Gotham, where Scup he consigned
To trusted, tried friend. At ease then in mind,
Also great elated, he returned to high chair
Selected to fill. 'Twas whilst reigning wise there
One day flashed by wire in cipher dispatch
That one David B. Hill had stolen Knight's catch
Conceal'd with such care. Knight storm'd, he yell'd, tore;
Pulled handsful of hair out; he thundered; howled, swore;
Then chartered car—parlor; in time very brief
Was he in New York on track of damned thief;
But all was in vain. But of this more at last, or
In Knight's manifesto, in war, or disaster.

Disdaining traditions, party practice, set rules,
Men one time his friends now treating as fools,
Knight, mounti'g stout bike, with good, sound rubber tire,
With Slupsky along for adviser, guide, squire,
Struck out for far West. But ere Fat Knight did so
He issued great, grand, deep, high manifesto.
It read: "To all nations, all peoples, all powers:
To all men athirst for reform such as ours:
Hear ye! Now Attend! For we, high Panjandrum,
Smite, beateth tomtom! Now sound loud alarum?
Scup Magic is missing! Dirty dog! Dastard!
Scoundrel base! Caitiff! Poltroon! Lousy bastard!

Rich treasure hath stolen! On isle of Manhattan
Is fiend intrenched; there quick we must at 'im!
But that is not all. Many wrongs now implore
Men pure, patriotic, to wage wholesome war.
All parties are putrid! Like herring shotten
Are houses, assemblies, grave senates—all rotten!
As declared profound Campbell, in his 'Civitas' song,
Through Anarchia's mouth, Whate'er is is wrong.
I hold to that doctrine, excepting, of course,
Myself, renowned Abe, grand elect of my force,
As Pod, Dink, Dome, Geza, Hoke, Snigg, some few more
Who think as I think, who sleep when I snore;
Who when I take snuff are all certain to sneeze;
To whom as gold idol they pray on their knees;
Who have sounded great depths of my political sea;
Behold me new Savior from new Galilee;
Bold St. John politic; strong Napoleon to soar—
To conquer all earth by appeal, or by war;
Another Columbus; second Lincoln to save
This planet from thralldom that doth her enslave;
Best teacher of teachers; wise Moses to guide;
Arch-goldbug of goldbugs; of Wall street chief pride;
Bright, pacifical Blaine, great Webster in reach
In powers perceptive, if not vocal speech;
Keén Randolph, sound Jay, cool Adams, high Hayne,
Loved Winkelried, Cæsar, Assarotti, Tom Paine,
Bacon, Praise Barebone, shrewd Barnum, brave Bayard,
Disraeli, Bellamy, Cheeshhahteaumuck, sired
Full-blooded Indian; J. Bentham, Schonhausen,
Ma-ka-tae-mish-kia-kiak, Morgan, Camphausen,
Blackstone, fon Blooker, Bolingbroke, Bolivar,
Bozzaries, George Brummel, J. Brutus, A. Oliver,
E. Burke, Cadoudal, Cagliostro, Chesterfield,
Cincinnatus, Hill Cobbett, Dick Cobden, Bill Enfield,
Crichton, Coke, Crispi, Old Noll, Davy Crockett,
Chatham, Clay, Clarendon, Thomas a Becket,
Chase, Johnny Churchill, Farragut, Tilden,
Tom Sackville, Steve Douglas, Duns Scotus, Milton,
Everett, Fessenden, Franklin, Godolphin,
Grant, Greeley, Grevy, great Larry Godkin,

Hon. W. L. Campbell.

Raider John Morgan.

Adolphus Gustavus, Hannibal, Hampden,
Halifax, Hancock, Alex Hamilton, Hampton,
Haroun-al-Raschid, Joe Hawley, Tom Hendricks;
Bill, Scott, Ben Harrison; Gottfried von Leibnitz,
George Frisbie Hoar, his great brother, E. Rockwood,
Lawyer, fine jurist; likewise, Belva Lockwood
With all of vast rest now holding high station
For goodness, or greatness, on earth, or in nation.
Whom you may pick out of list lengthy, rare,
In Webster's appendix, to with me compare,
For precious time flies; now nations in grief
Appeal nightly, day, for reform, quick relief,
Which full with my aid, Abe Slupsky, soon I
From 'Frisco on east shalt abundant supply,
Towns, cities, great states, convening en route,
Instructing, explaining; resolving acute
Plans deeply matured by myself daily, night,
All wrongs to remove, all mistakes to make right.
Awheel I shalt speed, adopting said plan,
A-ass, or ahorse, Slupsky, aid, in bike's van.
To show watching world that we who reform
Disdain not one whit with bike vogue to conform.
Besides, I expect to ride on at swift rate
Attracting attention—reducing my weight,
Thus killing two birds, as they say, with one stone.
As onward we triumph through temperate zone
Strewing glad tidings; enriching plagued poor;
Changing conditions far too hard to endure;
Scaling down taxes; spreading peace; proving gold
Catholicon full for all ills new, or old;
Advising reforms in regard to all crops,
As wheat, oats, alfalfa, hemp, rye, apples, hops,
Buckwheat, red clover, barley, hoop-poles, flitch, flax,
Hedges, rail fences, ditch-draining, ricks, stacks,
Soap-making, sow-gelding, corn-cutting, sap, bees,
Botts, glanders, footrot, spavins, hollow-horn, heaves,
Condescending to stoop as well as to soar!
As we sweep from wide West to rich Eastern shore.
I also invite to consult on long way
All true, tried reformers, hoping many shall stay,

Mrs. Dimmick's.

Becoming firm part of great army, or clan,
I purpose to form to regenerate man.
All men of all minds, all ye men of all creeds,
All men of all kinds, all ye men of all breeds,
All women, also; we extend invitation
To join us, to aid this vast demonstration
Expected—yea, destined—to thrill even Mars
As earth to foundation grand host we man jars.
Respond as I trust, come forth at this call,
Myself as your leader, with God over all,
Confiding in me, yet looking to Him,
With vigilance, valor, voice, vigor, vaunt, vim,
Provisions, rum, bedding, fresh meat, kola, salt.
To comfort, cheer, strengthen great hosts when we halt,
Or go into camp; then we shall succeed,
All earth making captive thro' our platform, speech, seed;
Not fierce like Mohammeds, nor Englands, who lord
O'er millions by logic of Maxim, troops, sword,
But like mild St. Patrick who plucked from green sod
Frail shamrock, converting Celt nation to God,
Who, plain truth to tell, despite Mick adhesion.
Hath often been shy with shot, rent, provision.
Come ye forth as one man! Come out of great wet!
Come on, Colonel Lease, thou once Populist pet!
Come, Jerry, of Kansas! Come whether stout pair
Of socks grace your feet, sir, or if they are bare!
Come, Debs, if you can! If still in cell pale
Get Altgeld to pardon, or demolish greed's jail.
Come, O'Donovan Rossa! Mad, if you wish, drag,
Cursing, fell spitting on, England's foul rag.
Come, Stone, of Missouri! Come, fetching your flights
Oratoric volcanic for cherished state's rights.
Come, Marshal Jo Shelby! Come under blurred bars
If still, Jo, at outs with Sam's stripes, burnished stars.
Come, Finerty, howling! An' whin yees come, John,
If yees so desire, dhrag domned Vic along!
Come, Mattie Pollard! Mat, too, when you come,
Be sure to fetch with you that pure 'Silver Tongue.'
Come, Denis Kearney! Come on with wide mouth!
Come, Tillman fierce, from your seat in suave South!

Tom.

Come, half of Chicago! Come State Street Van Pragg!
Come, Allerton, Darrow! Come, Altgeld! Don't lag!
Come, Morss, though in Paris! Come, Johnny McLane!
Come, Major McKinley! Tom Reed, haste from Maine!
Come, mailed, mighty Thoman! Fall in, mute Depew!
Come, Mr. Cal Brice! Come, be one of us, too!
Come, thirsty Herr Most! Come, Mr. Funk, join!
Come, Tammany Croker! Come Harvey with 'Coin!'
Come, honored Peffer, immortaled through hair!
Come, queen of Hawaii! Come! Cease to despair!
Come, Dana, even! Blaze along with hot Sun!
Come, Hesing! Come, Kohlsaat, who maketh brown bun!
Come, profound Morton! Come, come, Nalls—Ion B.!
Come, New Jersey Griggs! Come Gas Benedict—flee!
Come, Os Ottendofer! Come, every Cuckoo!
Come, Jaegerblut Damsen! Come, Goff! Come Garoo!
Come, Barber Raabe! Come, Ezekiel Hedges!
Come, Billy Brookfield! Come, Shiner with pledges!
Come, golden Carlisle! Come, be cogent arm!
Come, Tony Comstock, guarding off Pri'pus harm!
Come, perfect Parkhurst, with purity's shield!
Come, Weaver, who gallant before Libby kneeled!
Come, papal Satolli, with bull from blessed pope!
Come, Corrigan, bishop, with Irish soft-soap!
Come, mighty Lewelling, from near glaucous Kaw!
Come, Geza, Dink Botts! Come, Waite, bloody-raw!
Come, Pulitzer grand! Come Ingalls, so slim!
Come, Carl Browne! Come, Coxey! Come, bring others in!
Let A. P. A. come! All Hub free-thinkers, too;
Huns, Swedes, Poles, Italians, wild Irish, shrewd Jew,
Dudes, Turke, all New Women, skinflints, Javanese,
Mugwumps, dock-wollopers, all kickers, Chinese,
Swell Wallstreets, proud Goldbugs, Debsites, Yanks, strikers,
Sam Jones, DeWitt, jawsmiths, pistareens, pikers,
Rascals, knaves, Algers, fools, ragtag, touts, Pandars,
Peddlers, flim-flammers, tramps, porters, canners,
Fiddlers, wind-jammers, hams, hoboes, sitters,
Barflies, beats, hop-fiends, mugs, mashers, hitters,
Oscars, horse-rubbers, tin-horns, fault-finders,
Lunch-cutters, coons, cusses, cads, curs, high-binders,

Coin Harvey.

And so on and so forth and so forth and so on
Till there's no more riff-raff to come or go on,
And now for my plan: With such raw material,
High, low, politic, lay, ministerial,
We roll up our sleeves, as if to kneed dough—
When new Third-term party, behold you and lo!
Pure, high, noble, good, in all vast, varied mass
To mix in with riff-raff, debased, vulgar class,
Thus blending at last in grand polis machine
That wonder desired so—true, golden mean.
We'll gold have at bottom—gold have, too, at top;
Gold in all forms 'll be our principal crop,
So far as coin goes. With copper, cheap paper,
Wampum, vile silver, base latter West's caper,
We'll hold no communion, but grow vital, bold,
Wise, content, true, most just, with dear gold.
We'll wear yellow clothes; our wines shall be yellow;
Our books yellow-backs; each men yellow fellow;
Our flag shall be orange, but not to raise by it
Good Irish who join us to frenzy, mad riot,
But fully proclaim, by xanthical hue,
Gold yellow great god we all worship true.
We'll call, or I will, with trumpet or horn,
All people hereafter to raise yellow corn;
We'll try to arrange that but one disease,
That one yellow jaundice, shall make all decease.
But other main point—most vital of all—
To attention of cosmos again wouldst recall:
As many now know, I was lately despoiled
Of treasure for which I hard struggled, moiled,
To benefit all. To Scup Magic refer;
Faintest mention of outrage must coldest heart stir!
That wrong to avenge, that Scup to secure,
Methinks every nation any fate should endure.
But America sure, to which most I appeal,
Should hearken, quick act. Accoutred in steel,
With arms, stores, brave hosts I appeal to come
To follow my banner, directions, fife, drum.
Come patriots, rally! Come, as flocked Boys in Blue
When war tocsin sounded! When my substitute drew

My sword to save Union! Come, join me, Dink, Pod!
With others enlisted for my Scup, reform, God!
But no more in detail. I, closing, appeal,
Urge, implore, beg, entreat, all men when I wheel,
With Slupsky along, to join in with all might
Reform, Magic Scup, full to aid.

"The Fat Knight."

Manifesto spread broadcast, two billions or more,
From lakes down to gulf, from far West to East shore,
In Asia, in Europe, in China, Japan,
Australia—wherever high heaven breeds man—
Outlining long route, which will duly appear,
Affairs more important concerning us here,
Excited commotion, not alone in Sam's states,
But earth total throughout, inspiring debates,
Great meetings, conventions, mobs, manifests, calls,
Uprisings, excursions, bouts, barbecues, balls,
Afternoon teas, bazars, kettle-drums, dinners,
Camp-meetings for state, not unchristian sinners,
All races at once resolving to to fall in,
Affiliate with, catch on to, or crawl in,
For Knight's manifesto was writ in each tongue
God in His wisdom so diffusely hath hung
In mouths of all nations, when it seems diffusion
Keeps peoples apart, to say naught of confusion,
Misunderstanding, imposture, snare, devil,
All hell to pay, when extensive we travel.
Magazines, monthlies, weeklies, diurnals,
Broadsides, gazettes, heavy quarterlies, journals,
Books, volumes, tomes, sheets, dodgers, cards, pictures,
Periodicals, posters, cartoons, cuts, caricatures,
With everything man may depict or put ink on
To show how, or what, he ever may think on,
Blazed, boomed, boosted, lifted up, lauded,
Whoop-laed, hurrahed, ki-yied, yelled, applauded,
Puffed, urged, proclaimed, commanded, flare-headed,
Repeated, rehashed, re-rehashed, triple-leaded,
With such vim, vigor, vengeance, fast presses, pen,
Could never reveal to cool souls of sane men

Knight's whole manifesto for months five or six
In all kinds of type, in all styles most prolix,
As printed are platforms born every four years,
One side loud in praise, one set grinning jeers.
When highest was din Fat Knight, though wight single,
Inspired event making every ear tingle,
For word came by boat, was then flashed by wire,
That he in Hawaii had become regal sire
Of burnt-umber prince, murky mother, Queen Lil,
Conceiving, safe bearing, through miraculous will,
As didst spouse of Joseph, strange fact some assume,
As didst Thomas Paine, to gross, flippant impugn,
For naught is too pure, too good, grand, or great,
But Voltaires, Paines, Volneys, most vilely berate,
Exulting to find, not sweet fruit, finest bloom, [fume,
Meads, meadows, pink orchards, pine woods, prized per-
But swamps, pools, lagoons, miasma, pits dank,
Sand wastes, poisoned jungles, dirty ditches, smells rank,
As if filth mephitic more appealed to men's nose,
More satisfied soul, than sweet scent of rare rose.
Now little prince dark, bruno pride of pitch queen,
State policy's idol, when it time came to wean,
Most ravenous sucked; he stuck to brown dug
Like pup to gum root—udder closer didst hug.
Odd birth scandal bred, but bold father from youth,
Admiring justice, brave declared "Tell the truth!"
That candidly done, his fame great wider spread;
Thick, fast to his standard from all points purists sped,
Men saying with pride, as some foes didst him truss,
"He is a grand leader, for sure he's like us!"
But abroad very different. All o'er, around, earth,
Except here at home, as in land of babe's birth,
Cooled respect for Fat Knight; some, too, even went
So far as to spit on his flag with contempt,
But his Mugwumps stood firm like many more, too,
Much warmed by his sunshine, refreshed by his dew,
To his support rushing, which seeing, Fat Knight,
Having sympathy deep, clear observing new light
All earth needed sadly, praised manifest quilled;
Then, per his order, all earth dark was billed,

With directions minute as to how he'd proceed,
What cities go through, when speak, repose, feed;
How long remain here, how long operate there; [mayor;
When bands could him welcome; if he'd visit town's
What wheel Knight would ride; just how he would ride it;
When Slupsky should lead, or ass ride beside it;
When balloons would ascend; when guns might be fired;
When gyasticutus could be seen, if desired,
With all other detail, which needen't be hinted,
Since, as you all know, 'twas repeatedly printed,
Whilst our valuable space, so much agate square,
As dailies would tell you, we at present can't spare,
For we should not conceal, some papers have sires,
Great editors, even, who're occasionally liars.
Indeed, some've aver'd, but base scound'ls were caught up,
That editors actually once could be bought up,
For earth teems with falsehood; no faultless McLean,
Bill Brown, Godkin, Reid, may escape venomed stain.
Fair heights lure men low, who exultantly sing
If bring down fine eagle. When success sweeps awing
In splendor at noonday in pure, ambient air,
Black, foul, carrion ravens are croaking somewhere;
Jays some place are screaming; too, somewhere tomtit,
Shrill magpie, small peewee, are flirting flat wit.
Curs hate noble mastiff; men, too, may be found
So unreasonably hating their betters. Good hound
Is Chevalier Bayard compared with mean soul,
Which must be so small as deep eye of chuff mole,
E'er viewing with malice, with scorn, lethal hate,
Deep, damnable envy, true worth of men great.
Yet some are so sordid. Some, e'en, are such curs
They turn up their nose when judgment lauds Schurz;
Some down so have fallen they poison distil,
With wink, innuendo, when Buffalo Bill
Praise loudly applauds. Some, too, with scoff, sneer,
Names Dismuke, Bine, Suggs, Koozer, Castellane hear;
Laugh loud at Dink Botts; e'en shake in gross glee
When Slupsky, Snigg, Hoke, famed statesmen, they see
In Dana's Sun lauded. How malice, fell hate,
Damned envy, pursue, lethal plague mortals great!

Such, too, morals' status now here in base land
That, some shouting "Cleveland!" others yell "He be
damned!"
Hence, then can you marvel when editors pure,
So incorrupt, chaste, whom naught e'er could allure,
Unsullied, untainted, untarnished, clean,
Immaculate, holy like virtue's pure queen,
Innocent, guileless, solert, fine, fair,
Faultless, unblemished, kind, consummate, rare,
Sound, certain, blameless, lucrific, complete,
Finished, accomplished, effective, replete,
Suitable, clever, skilled, competent, able,
Adapted, outspoken, high, capable, stable,
Neat, able-minded, powerful, vigorous;
Aboveboard, abluent, astral, crucigerous,
Absolute, qualified, non-relative, right,
Self-sufficing, abstemious, temperate, bright,
Abstinent, glorious, continent, gracious,
Abstracted, abstruse, superb, veracious,
Copious, classic, abundant, consistent,
Fulminant, self-restraining, wak'ning, persistent,
Acataleptic, academic acute,
Keen, scholarly, subtile, alert, resolute,
Adjudicative, persevering, precise,
All-powerful, just, energetic, sharp, nice,
Vernant, acopic, sagacious, incisive,
Sharp-witted, hypnotic, adjustive, decisive,
Lively, prompt, centric, Achillean, affable,
Acceptable, civil, lawyerly, laughable,
Accompletive, chronical, acologic, profound,
Invincible, adequate, upright, renowned,
Æsthetic, appeasive, apropos, meet,
Pleasing, smooth, elegant, deft, nonpareil, sweet,
Ardent, sweet-scented, eager, soncy, intense,
Pindaric, antalgic, fond, loving, immense,
Courteous, stately, universal, benign,
Condesending, accessible, stimulative, ashine,
Radiant, striking, tender, affectional,
Alexipyretic, devoted, exceptional,
Allegiant, amphibious, peaceable, seasonable,
Altruistic, beneficent, unselfish, reasonable,

Antisyphilitic, answerless, careful,
Antaphroditic, warm, fervid, prayerful,
Amenable, lovable, vivific, sprightly,
American, versal, armipotent, knightly,
All-seeing, arousing, androgynous, beautiful,
Antibilious, embrosian, delicious, pat, dutiful,
Antilithic, adroit, befitting, Æonian,
Anthelmintic, expositive, scholastic, Adonean,
Complaisant, athletic, beneficial, affectible,
Earnest, diffluent, welcome, delectable,
Antidysenteric, antedeluvial,
Scaturiginous, antiscorbutical,
Shrewd, jocund, watchful, aristocratic,
Prudent, desirable, expert, axiomatic,
Ambaginous, charming, antisceptical, loyal,
Agreeable, amiable, irresistible, royal,
Advisory, adjuvant, administerial,
Æstuous, Æsopic, advancive, aerial,
Aristophanic, indorsable, fearless,
Stout-hearted, high-minded, Chesterfieldian, peerless,
Brobdingnagian, bully, resplendent, concise,
Cavalier, worshipful, wonderful, wise,
Divertive, God-fearing, monitive, sociable,
Pungent, pure, noteworthy, museful, cognocible,
Right-hearted, reciprocous, gladsome, perfective,
Free-handed, galliard, convenient, corrective,
Uttermost, credent, uncommon, safe, wealthy,
Well-favored, quintessential, puissant, healthy,
Gamogenetic, decretive, expressive,
Conjubilant, sparkling, cultured, progressive,
Platycephlous, mild, plausible, regnant,
Purposeful, quiddative, radious, pregnant,
Luciferous, lyric, lenitive, lawful,
Hyperion, honest, Argus-eyed, awful,
Long-headed, valid, petrifical, memorable,
Unbiased, virile, virtuous, venerable,
Punctilious, pushing, plain-hearted, perfusive,
Subsecutive, solid, decided, exclusive,
Brave, hemathermal, hospitable, healing,
Fletiferous, first-rate, fecund, fresh, feeling,
Star-spangled, stanch, satisfactory, votive,
Gymnorhinal, grandific, guidable, fotive,
Hermenuetical, glad, good-tempered, glowing,
Foresighted, high-mettled, deep, kingly, knowing,
Instructional, lion-like, luxive, comeatable,
Subderisorious, magic, compatible,
Behooveful, composed, collegiate, burning,
Clear-seeing, distinguished, dynamic, discerning,
Consentient, exhaustive, dilucid, cyclonic,
Expetible, sensuous, easeful, Byronic,
Bountiful, bouncing, convivial, beauteous,
High-spirited, dexterous, diligent, duteous,
Dolichocephalic, eagle-eyed, dashing,
Consuetudinal, exculpable, flashing,
Trumpet-tongued, waxing, well-informed, spotless,
Theurgic, thoughtful, veridical, blotless,

Explicit, high-hearted, honorable, blooming,
Hortative, high-born, historical, booming,
Adventurous, jovial, bookful, forgiving,
Aristotelic, bicrural, lawgiving,
Antephialtic, argumentative, boon,
Discriminating, unconfined, opportune,
Circumspect, clement, bewitching, Miltonic,
Amaranthine, compunctive, docent, harmonic,
Strengthening, boundless, admonitive, gregal,
Affectionate, blissful, chivalric, regal,
Catastaltic, cathartic, blessed, munific,
Anthropical, bribeless, august, terrific,
Alexipharmic, acquisitive, lucky,
Centicipitous, anthophorous, plucky,
Endeictic, exalted, gerent, pubescent,
Debonair, dainty, extant, reminiscent,
Assonant, brilliant, pious, aligerous,
Halcyon, haloed, heteronymous, generous,
Forensical, handsome, encouraging, critical,
Genuine, gilt-edged, favored, political,
Matchless, meracious, overwhelming, reprieving,
Inscrutable, piquant, microdont, relieving,
Picturesque, placid, pedestaled, probal,
Panurgic, persisting, obligable, noble,
Remarkable, ravishing, proverbial, settled,
Refreshing, refined, magnifiable, mettled,
Isapostolic, virent, omniscious,
Intrepid, lasting, legitimate, precious,
Receptible, witty, diamantiferous,
Talented, hylic, candent, thuriferous,
Senseful, superior, spirited, splendid,
Singular, sinless, sincere, serene, well-bred,
Transporting, traveled, tranquil, favonian,
Vivid, victorious, vast, Jeffersonian,
Socratic, solacious, strenuous, pabulous,
Patronal, Spartan, superexcellent, fabulous,
Univocal, upright, unerring, productive,
Various, vital, sublunar, seductive,
Strong-minded, studious, self-possessed, truthful,
Scrupulous, suasive, tested, triumphal,
Time-honored, touching, undauntable, fitted,
Suspectless, symmetric, symbolic, quick-witted,
Tralatitious, aseptic, signal, consoling,
Stainless, sublime, transplendent, condoling,
Volitient, auctive, artistic, judicious,
Authoschediastic, exulting, auspicious,
Icarian, imposing, important, peloric,
Impeccant, incentive, catholic, caloric,
Coherent, massive, saturient, Dantean,
Cogent, colossal, circumfluent, gigantean,
Belgravian, docile, hallowed, retiring,
Poculent, comely, cherubic, aspiring,
Terrible, lofty, Euclidian, notable,
Empyreal, concordant, quadrable, quotable,
Prophoric, regardful, reliable, funny,
Quotidian, solvent, rhetoric, ripe, sunny,

Purgative, punctual, princely, particular,
Approvable, apposite, armored, apicular,
Especial, compunctious, crebrous, Platonic,
Deified, sacred, superhuman, Laconic,
Constructive, best, dulcet, cornucopian,
Conservative, bold, extra, cyclopean,
Dolichocephalous, depthless, anetic,
Executorial, expeditious, eupeptic,
Convictive, courtly, crowned, independent,
Cutting, courageous, cosmic, resplendent,
Entrancing, experienced, contubernal, chief,
Esemplastic, distinctive, viripotent, brief,
Tutorial, timely, tolerant, very,
Theochristic, unbane, unparalleled, merry,
Winsome, well, weighty, unfailing, capacious,
Unimpeachable, utter, volant, edacious,
Thaumaturgical, calm, statarian, blushing,
Straightforward-spoken, stoical, rushing,
Tempting, Herculean, tenable, trusty,
Expiscatory, demotic, good, lusty,
Deictic, enchanting, fair-minded, tectonic,
Epexegetic, beloved, amphigonic,

Benignant, good-humored, forbearant, brotherly,
Fissiped, gamic, germane, gifted, motherly,
Sanctified, saintly, rapturous, thunderous,
Radiant, rousing, quodlibetical, wonderous,
Entheastic, good-natured, gnomical, believable,
Fibrochondrosteal, labent, achievable,
Heterogeneous, huge, Ciceronian,
Gustable, graceful, famous, Catonian,
Dapatical, fathomless, gorgeous, expanding,
Enthymematic, fertile, commanding,
Felicitous, deathless, humane, mirific,
Glittering, graphic, benedictive, specific,
Entertaining, great-hearted, sovereign, gregarious,
Surpassing, true-blue, thearchic, vicarious,
Timocratic, terse, calefacient, engaging,
Attollent, attractive, assuring, assuaging,
Scaturient, scintillant, humanitarian,
Vigilant, ortive, staid, sanitarian,
Tangible, tasteful, back-boned, effulgent,
Teleorganic, unassuming, indulgent,
Superlative, thrall-less, exercent, wiry,
Thankworthy, total, terrestrial, fiery,
Alterative, armed, buoyant, emulsive,
Unlimited, cherished, pretty, divulsive,
Promethean, psychal, philanthropical,
Purificative, rich, theanthropical,
Quick, quaquaversal, propice, opiferous,
Relieful, reformed, rising, pedigerous,
Pyrophorous, potent, provident,palpebrate,
Proleptic, respectful, readable, accurate,
Relevant, rightful, blithe, arenaceous,
Responsible, requisite, enough, pertinacious,
Religious, salvific, right-minded, polemic,
Prevenient, poetic, quick-sighted, the'remic,

Ponderous, popular, game, consequential,
Flexanimous, sabulous, smart, penitential,
Successful, suffisant, trim, oratorian,
Mature, meritorious, ornate, senatorian,
Infinite, odorous, borborygmal, unfettered,
Reserved, inchuretic, agminal, lettered,
Dirigent, drastic, encyclic, advisable,
Convellent, corporeal, conformable, prizable,
Unequaled, unceasing, serious, clergical,
Sensitive, sensible, statesmanlike, surgical,
Sapientious, satiric, self-evident, gentle,
Sharp-sighted, sciential, adminicular, mental,
Effluvial, feal, susceptible, conticent,
Sensiferous, Tempean, testable, eminent,
Kaleidoscopic, imperturbable, fateful,
Intuitional, lavish, inflexible, grateful,
Miraculous, pertinent, pellucid, evident,
Peaceful, peculiar, omniferous, reverent,
Panivorous, plentiful, scissible, measureless,
Normal, plethoric, original, marvelous,
Plenipotentiary, mighty, multipotent,
Merciful, palpable, modest, pauciloquent,
Yearnful, ascensive, transcendent, inspiring,
Supereminent, sipid, shining, inquiring,
Autogentic, tenacious, stylish, percutient,
Sedative, seemly, soothing, discutient,
Unequivocal, wholesome, wide, comprehensible,
Significant, sophic, spicy, subsensible,
Versatile, well-read, syllogistical, gratified,
Valorous, valuable, undeniable, ratified,
Steadfast, substantive, autog'mous, zetetic,
Zealotic, domestic, strict, diuretic,
Ubiquitous, trustful, suitable, meritable,
Unapproachable, thinking, true-hearted, veritable,
High-spirited, lambent, alacrious, breezy,
Armisonant, clysmic, inspiriting, easy,
Anagogical, cautious, cardinal, active,
Electric, effable, true-born, didactive,
Diversiloquent, dynastic, conclusive,
Full, constitutional, doughty, diffusive,
Homogeneous, feat, honey-tongued, prominent,
Homiletic, heroic, habitual, dominant,
Feasible, fellowless, frugiferous, sightly,
Logical, literate, lovely, almighty,
Limitless, limpid, live, lordly, deserving,
Luxurious, laureled, lion-hearted, preserving,
Imperscrutable, manful, experient,
Incontestable, balsamic, aperient,
Conceptible, expedite, philoprogenitive,
Continual, contrite, hale, supersensitive,
Exhilarant, findy, exuperant, ready,
Fatiloquent, favorite, flammiferous, steady,
Largifical, well-born, winning, eternal,
Voluminous, peptic, auspicial, supernal,
Armigerous, capital, hallelujatic,
Antemundanean, celestial, emphatic,

Succinct, celebrated, beatific, elective,
Conservative, costly, radicated, reflective,
Antemetic, adept, exegetic, advisable,
Cosmopolite, crescive, equicrure, cognizable,
Cool, democratic, republican, national,
Constructive, fiducial, epenetical, rational,
Munificent, mordant, model, essential,
Methodic, mentorial, metaphysic, potential,
Prosimetrical, prosperous, erudite,
Proletaneous, prophylactical, recondite,
Salubrious, sapient, respectable, alible,
Righteous, resourceful, calid, infallible,
Seminal, stalwart, allochroic, emotive,
Antarthritic, alive, eristic, denotive,
Compensative, cognitive, evincive, detective,
Dispassionate, congruous, consultive, directive,
Inpartial, inductive, lucid, devotional,
Inexhaustive, industrious, lifesome, emotional,
Perpetuate, paramount, ovant, conversive,
Orologic, orderly, mittent, discursive,
Momentous, mnemonic, painstaking, eventful,
Perennial, pervasive, perficient, contentful,
Orthomorphic, obliging, gritty, explorable,
Ontologic, pedarian, patriotic, adorable,
Palatial, pandemic, first-class, Apollonian,
Omnipercipient, pensive, Baconian,
Persistive, persuasive, patient, evincible,
Orthodox, optimate, organic, convincible,
Permanent, perfect, sepelible, meedful,
Mundificant, pithful, penetrant, heedful,
Paradigmatical, menticultural, leading,
Perpendicular, chipper, orectic, exceeding,
Approachable, caustic, Christian, deific,
Delenifical, dichromatic, magnific,
Elysian, disquisitive, piteous, factual,
Elenctic, excerptive, exoterical, actual,
Dioristic, vehement, evolutional, flourishing,
Dulcifluous, fleckless, fastidious, nourishing,
Epigrammatic, free, pulchritudinous,
Enthusiastic, stout, multitudinous,
Foresighted, facile, extraregular, numerous,
Fortitudinous, equiponderous, humorous,
Decorous, dependable, equable, pleasurable,
Professorial, decent, immeasurable,
Fulcible, hospital, gamesome, omnific,
Open, Epictetian, frigefactive, pacific,
Definable, pistic, epidictical, dear,
Imperatorial, immutable, clear,
Worthy, lawmaking, mannerly, credible,
Inconceivable, geldable, regible,
Advanced, gratifying, cheerful, prudential,
Aetheogamus, anecdotal, parentrl,
Medicinal, sorbile, noctilucous, conservant,
Pantascopic, pan'cean, plain-spoken, observant,
Manifold, pluperfect, percipient, hustling,
Phenomenal, placable, luminous, bustling,

Instructive, ingenuous, becoming, conceptive,
Obedient, brightest, discoursive, receptive,
Theopathic, traductive, tragic-comic, concussive,
Unalloyed, understanding, undoubted, discussive,
Segregate, searching, sejant, perspicacious,
Systematical, splendrous, fraught, efficacious,
Contented, exempt, free-hearted, commendable,
Consonant, entheal, full-blooded, dependable,
Solicitous, dirigible, docible, beaming,
Contemplant, sejungible, featurely, teeming,
Fructiculose, harborous, extemporaneous,
Incontaminate, goodly, subtegulaneous,
Sugescent, sumless, sorted, estiferous,
Epencephalic, equanimous, etherous,
Alepidote, occupied, animative, exciting,
Amphigean, archical, blooded, delighting,
Catagmatic, commonitive, appropriate, bland,
Advantageous, assiduous, aptitudinal, grand,
Dispositive, conscionable, incomprehensible,
Federate, fumigant, indeprehensible,
Furthersome, obvious, gainful, extatic,
Forcible, fulgid, epanthous, auxetic,
Entitative, finiteless, informative, excellent,
Interpretative, latitudinous, crepitant,
Jurisprudent, intrinsic, incitant, affluent,
Illustrious, imponderous, inerrable, confident,
Invaluable, lustrous, instant, deviceful,
Indefeasible, level, intelligent, spiceful,
Luminiferous, luscious, jalapic, omnipotent,
Insurmountable, macrotous, bellipotent,
Ornamental, pecunious, motive, feracious,
Exemplary, heavenly, festal, vivacious,
Perfervid, placentious, plangentical, eloquent,
Philosophic, ostensible, plenary, refulgent,
Alleviative, chrestomathic, efficient,
Apprecatory, consultive, proficient,
Contiguous, pacate, coprolitic, paternal,
Dichotomous, coruscant, far-sighted, fraternal,
Inerratic, indubious, killing, unhurtful,
Imperial, incessant, influential, desertful,
Investigative, indagative, coysome,
Inconfutible, pachydermatous, joysome,
Ordinant, leonine, mindful, protective,
Pancratic, perpetual, playful, projective,
Platycephalic, large, macrocephalous,
Imperdible, levigate, precellent, affabrous,
Polymathic, profulgent, instinct, diplomatic,
Protreptical, primal, promotive, pragmatic,
Providential, full-fledged, vestal, benevolent,
Epagogic, precantal, candid, altivolant,
Expedient, fervid, fatherly, pensative,
Indefective, lucific, indicative, pulsative,
Anurous, eligible, executive, ethical,
Impressible, indicant, manifest, thetical,
Consolatory, invariable, mightful,
George-Washingtonian, gnostic, delightful,

BULLETIN.

Murdered in Cold Blood.

Scandal in High Life.

Rape of Ten Tender Virgin

Rattling, Artistic Cock Figt

Screaming, Salacious Divorce

Minister Arrested for Seducti

Intrigue of Senator So-and-S

Fornication Terminates in Ter Tragedy.

Fall of a Deacon from Grac

Complete Roster of Europe's B Bastards.

Sensation, Spice, Vice and Inf

See the Daily Sewer-Pipe!

Cent a Copy! 3c a Week!

Our Motto: Let no Scandal Es

Charismatic, substantial, encyclopedic,
Theandric, enforcive, ethopoetic,
Sabatic, festivous, formful, detergent,
Fragrant, fructiferous, handy, abstergent,
Iconoclastic, ignoscible, consecrate,
Irreproachable, likely, elaborate,
Macrencephalic, intact, amatorian,
Philopolemical, imperatorian,
Patrician, moliminous, overt, transparent,
Periastral, plain-dealing, daring, concurrent,
Philharmonic, praiseworthy, evangelistic,
Preeminent, privileged, philanthropistic,
Prepossessing, concinnous, hygienic, conducing,
Logographic, inuncted, inventive, seducing,
Maicutical, premial, content, sympathetic,
Sterling, conglutinant, edifying, syncretic,
Generic,genial, enterprising, sedate,
Indescribable, wide-spread, open-handed, elate,
Parenetic, omniscient, pabular, patible,
Persuadable, permeant, pleasant-tongued, vatical,
Sanguigenous, lenient, intellectual willing,
Eleutheromaniac, immatchable, thrilling,
Invigorating, esteemable, sumptuous,
Sectorial, preputial, sarcotic, unctuous,
Flavorous, fruitive, spontaneous, terrorless,
Gentilitious, ingredient, long-sighted, errorless,
Incomparable, imperant, succulent,
Selenocentric, incessible, luculent,
Inexhaustible, emulous, audible,
Intumulated, indeciduous, laudable,
Juristic, idoneous, illapsable, straight,
Introspective, inviolate, likeable, great,
Jocoserious, indefectible, legal,
Inexterminable, large-hearted, peregal,
Inoffensive, Ionic, intumescent, select,
Ingenious, interesting, irenic, elect,
Overawful, self-active, recreative, magnetic,
Mellow, multiscious, recollective, majestic,
Propulsive, protracted, preponderant, real,
Predictive, profluent, profusive, ideal,
Representative, Marcian, obtable, fluent,
Resuscitative, reviving, congruent,
Recompensive, sap'ential, prescious, enticing,
Prevalent, promising, sanguine, sufficing,
Recommendable, public, reflecting,unanimous,
Propitious, priceless, mitigative, magnanimous,
Philological, persant, relucent, angelic,
Sative, enchorac, diuturnal, selenic,
Disciplinary, educational, brightsome,
Confutative, scious, gentle-hearted, delightsome,
Equanimous, governing, fulgent, convincible,
Semeiological, fashionable, principal,
Serotinous, shotted, offenseless, conjugial,
Omniparous, neighborly, coroneted, connubial,
Exogamous, exorable, determinate, deputable,
Equilibrious, general, reparative, reputable,

Retrospective, resurgent, recipient, jubilant,
Pulmoniferous, psychagogic, predominant,
Reformatory, pregrogatived, delicate,
Polymorphous, polite, presentative, depurate,
Provocative, sanative, salient, enduring
Prodigious, promissive, telluric, alluring,
Archetypical, prime, irrefragable,
Crisp, captivating, first, indefatigable,
Apician, aviseful, basilic, insistent,
Rolant, arresting, unappalling, increscent,
Saturnian, special, hearty, deliberate,
Sapphic, erect, eviternal, considerate,
Alepidote, applicative, rosy, exuberant,
Examplary, frightless, forehanded, edulcorant,
Flexicostate, correct, intent, realistic,
Instrumental, preceptive, through, Jehovistic,
Antidotal, controllable, current, expectant,
Confidential, egregious, read, disinfectant,
Fundamental, facundious, hardy, ententive,
Epinicial, farraginous, fascinating, extensive,
Enubilous, equitable, culminant, learnable,
Diorthotic, fixed, forthright, frequent, discernible,
Eleatic, elenchical, feateous, lucrative,
Guaniferous, gustful, congenial, palative,
Conscientious, express, friendly, constrainable,
Nervous, defensive, rutilant, explainable,
Philotechnical, frank, ineradicable,
Elucidative, demulcent, irrejectable,
Hortensial, hodiernal, highmost, innocuous,
Hereditary, extramundane, multiloquous,
Salivant, sober, technologic, benefic,
Typical, trenchant, trusting, energetic,
Autogenous, sexual, proficuous, cheering,
Orphic, ostiferous, beamy, endearing,
Indulgent, kind-hearted, lentous, inspired,
Liberal, learned, lawabiding, admired,
Inimitable, pitiful, nitid, sensific,
Noological, physical, divine, scientific,
Illecebrous, loveful, corymbiferous,
Opulent, tutelar, odd, salutiferous,
Storied, excusable, hopeful, uniting,
Communicative, even-handed, inviting,
Fortunate, gainsome, indisputable,
Extraordinary, bracing, indubitable,
Behoovable, counselable, balmy, melodious,
Cordial, exact, instinctive, commodious,
Restorative, prizable, thankful, performable,
Elemental, prepared, public-hearted, reformable,
Biddable, bosom, gallant, transpicuous,
Exportable, fructuous, headmost, conspicuous,
Complimental, imaginous, busy, immensive,
Latreutical, favorable, incomprehensive,
Deiparous, ermined, happy, grammatical,
Heavenly-minded, helpful, plasmatical,
Dipyrenous, supportful, heartsome, doniferous,
Enjoyable, oily, gamy, pruniferous,

Conversible, luminant, grave, monumental,
Metalogical, mitigant, emolumental,
Observational, pleasant, ineffable,
Omnifarious, organific, inevitable,
Illuminant, operative, wonted, retentive,
Noetic, omnigenous, pithy, intentive,
Overcoming, multanimous, mollifiable, arduous,
Reciprocal, profitable, positive, sedulous,
Preparative, president, prelal, inspective,
Prevoyant, prepollent, caller, erective,
Convertible, predicant, precipient, pointed,
Practical, praisable, polished, anointed,
Regular, proper, away-up, parturient,
Prenuncious, night-blooming, sage, Epicureant,
Proficuous, practive, poignant, endemic,
Proceleusmatic, extreme, ecumenic,
Effectuous, heedy, patent, pennipotent,
Noumenal, all-right, egal, plenipotent,
Expressible, warning, self-reliant, eclectic,
Unexceptionable, meditative, di'lectic,
Immarcescible, true, eucharistic,
Sheeny, presentable, gay, euphemistic,
Titanic, tiptop, Godlike, tremendous,
Superangelic, everlasting, stupendous,
Impressive, immortal, above-intellectual,
Christly, supreme, by-great-God-Almightial,
Are slandered, traduced, abused, rank belied,
Kicked sometimes, rough cuffed, base spat on beside?
But Fat Knight, reformer, our high, holy hero,
You think we neglect? Quite likely. We fear so.
You're burning to see brave Knight in bright armor
For Scup—reform—fighting for all from poor farmer
To blacksmith, cook, painter, hostler, shoemaker,
Fisherman, tailor, teamster, clerk, baker,
Brushmaker, barber, potter, musician,
Porter, domestic, policeman, optician,
Bricklayer, butcher, cigarmaker, moulder,
Carpenter, peddler, news-agent, folder,
Plumber, reporter, jockey, fruit-vender,
Sailor, hack-driver, glazier, bartender,
Stonemason, waiter, book-keeper, welder,
Auctioneer, author, miner, sow-gelder;
You're anxious, we know, to see son of Cæsar
Afield with bold aids in blood to their knees, or
Hewing base foe, as at Tours, or Lepanto;
Therefore, invite you to taste final canto.

CONQUESTS WITH MARVELOUS WIND-UP.

Fat Knight afield; main actions there;
His dress, arms, wheel, odd helmets rare;
Great friends, fierce foes, reforms, en route
From 'Frisco east; Abe, aids, chiefs, suit;
Prized Magic Scup; fell, final fight
Where blood surged deep—grand triumphed Knight.

REVELATIONS.

CANTO III.

JULY 4 is peerless. With cannon, fife, drum,
Flags, bathos, orations, fireworks, marching, rum,
Fights, racing, picnics, proudest day of all year
About 65,000,000 observe, joy, revere.
Decoration day hallowed, when homage decks grave
Of Confederate Gray, true Union Blue brave,
Is meet, solemn, sacred. Glad Christmas all know,
With feasting, reunions, gifts, love, mistletoe,
Slings, beer, punches, cocktails, ale, prime whisky neat,
With slathers of all that is best for to eat,
Is held finest day, very merriest time,
In calendar put. In prose, prayer, pleasing rhyme,
Merry Christmas is lauded, warm welcomed, e'er blessed,
As tender, benevolent, happiest, best.
So it's been in long past, but never more Fourth
Can noisy appeal to South, East, West, chill North;
Nor can Decoration still bring gracious tear
To Columbia's eye, nor kind Christmas so cheer,
Since calendar now is high honored, most bright,
Patriotical, grand, sacred, glad, out-of-sight,
Through one rubric day more revered than rare three,
Or all year's remainder, through Fat Knight's decree
High ordaining that day when he, armed, awheel
Sped on for all nations' reform, fullest weal.
He stole forth in night dark. He thus sneaked away
To 'scape acclamations so certain if day
His departure had witnessed. Though proudest Knight,
In acclaim, noise, display, he found no delight;
So he sly forth incog, as some still declare
Slunk Lincoln when riding to executive chair.
Knight turned his face westward; hard rode day, as night,
Till ocean Pacific, Golden Gate, met his sight;
Then went into 'Frisco. There early next morn
He fleet forth awheel, in left hand monster horn.
Behind Slupsky rode, famed Abe of St. Louis,
Whose mount was fat ass, which proved as true ass

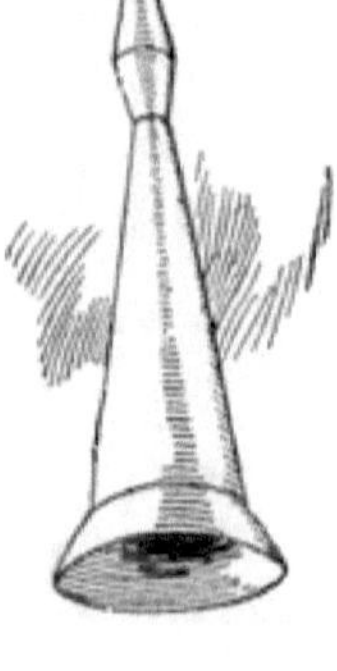

As ever saw Spain, ate pine knot, bull-thistle.
Abe, likely in jest, called ass he rode Bissle.
Whole outfit was yellow—yea, even Knight's horn,
Full six feet in length, was straw-color, or corn.
Fat Knight's face was hidden in mask he deft made
By splitting plump pumpkin huge thro' with sharp blade,
Orange guts scooping out, just leaving tough rind
To fit to round, fat face—tie, too, fast behind.
Two holes small for eyes, with horizontal, large hole,
Knifed in for Knight's mouth, made Knight appear droll,
Some boys crying "False face!" whilst others "Police!"
But Abe frowned upon them—then, lo, profound peace!
Abe also threw bills to his left, behind, right,
Apprising vast throng of full aim of Fat Knight,
Who that day in 'Frisco so gracious extolled
They meant in his honor to build shaft of gold;
One never of silver, base metal Fat Knight
Disdained like hell's devil—fought hard with much might.
But ere we describe Knight's achievements in war,
Let's advert to his wheel, with those things rare he wore,
In detail exact that Mulvaneys who limn
May paint, if inclined, true portrait of him.
Knight wore stiff sou'wester, best hat for foul weather,
Springing from top yellow rooster's tail feather;
Not broad leaf of cabbage, which libel maintains
Much lesser knight wore to protect superb brains.
Hat met helmet tough, which above we described,
Fitting perfect before, whilst firm behind tied.
Next his skin, we are told, Fat Knight's underclothes
Were fully as fine as Depew's, silk, or those
Of Swell Berry Wall. Knight's shirt was of wool—
Very long spreading tail, every place very full;
As ample, perhaps, as robe Webb for Chauncey
Dispatched special train for, so much did Peach fancy
That garment snowy—as immaculate quite
As robes angels sleep in near throne in bright night.
Knight's garment outside was all made in one piece,
Enveloping loosely brave Knight's form obese,
Which had puffed appearance; much seemed to assume
Contour, hue, extent, of stunted balloon
With head at tiptop, with pair bulky of legs
Sticking out at bulged sides. Attached to Knight's pegs,
Like body rotund encased in oiled stuff
As stout as sou'wester, were canvas shoes tough;
Broad belt 'round waist ample didst scarcely compress
Knight's serviceable, novel, most picturesque dress,
Which at one side supported broad, thick, lethal sword,
In dimentions with Knight made full to accord.
Dread sword was of metal—made likewise of wood;
For cutting, or bruising, was equally good,
One side being round, other side being made so
'Twould cleave through hard skull of toughest Thug,
jade, foe.

Smooth, round side was whiteoak, but t'other was made
Of finest of metal in Toledo steel blade.
Knight also'd odd gun. Its length was three feet,
At mouth bulging out. When shot off fan sheet
Of flame mixed with bullets piled pain, death, dismay,
Perhaps o'er full acre; gun, too, 'd hold at bay
Large farmyards of pullets; likewise, slick as grease,
Kill incredible numbers of ducks, turkeys, geese.
Knight, too, had keen dagger, completing fell store
Of weapons he carried to wage wanton war.
His wheel was stanch Safety which rose to great height,
Putting nine feet from earth fair, famous Fat Knight,
Who, as bike exalted could not for him kneel,
High step-ladder used when mounting huge wheel,
Which was brightest yellow, as also fat ass
Daring Slupsky bestrode, both pride of their class.
Abe dressed much like chief, except that Abe carried
Huge shield—immense cheese—with which he deft parried
Such missiles as eggs, rotten apples, cats, so on,
Small boys, depraved toughs, along route had thrown.
Abe sat up majestic. He seemed to reveal
Importance grave, deep, every squire must feel;
Not chunky, like Sancho, nor thin, like Spain's knight,
But in bone, flesh, in blood, for position just right.
Handbills disbursing, Abe'd occasionally shout,
"Men, come to great meeting! Good people, turn out!
Come, hear true reform! Come, hear Knight expound
His great principles plain, but nothing profound.
Come, men, women, children! For I tell you sincere,
'Tis last time Fat Knight in your midst will appear,
For thence we go East—yea, trip may extend
Across broad Atlantic—yea, farthermost end
Of wide, waning planet, which Fat Knight wouldst save
From argentine rascal, from white-metal knave!" [whack,
Someone threw red brickbat, which smote with loud
Abe taking unfairly in small of broad back,
Loose jarring fat kidneys. Bat, too, hit Abe's ass,
Who, kicking, retorted, but let retort pass,
Since beast's blast was rude, being hardly polite
For fair ladies to read, or gentlemen write.
Abe coarse yelled prolific oaths raising men's hair,
Beginning fierce combat to wage dreadful there,
When police interfered, stout pair on each side;
They stemmed war, rebellion, much slaughter beside,
For Fat Knight had pointed huge, bulging-mouthed gun,
Which soon would have started red rivers to run.
With vast concourse behind, to station bold two
Were taken, Knight making full statement plain, true,
Securing release; having, also, to boot,
So he said, full foundation for big damage suit

A Nonpareil.

Against San Francisco, but never to court
Went Knight with complaint on account of 'leged tort,
But great, grand, forgiving, invited them all
To follow to hear him expound wise in hall,
Where at night he addressed, with manifest gusto,
Men, women, children, of fine San Francisco,
His burning words wisest exciting applause
Ascending to heaven in reform's noble cause.
He said: "I adjure you—aye, friends, I exhort—
Ne'er bite ye in pickles displaying e'er wart!
Such impugn civil service—may, too, contravene
International law far worse than white bean
In Boston loved idol, though ever inclined,
When eaten by man, to large generate wind [smooth.
(Loud cheers, long huzzas). Men, your pickles have
Quite hard, brittle, dark-green. I never approve
Cucumbers pot-bellied, with paunch, or contour,
As in aldermen tough men are forced to endure.
Beware, too, of mixed pickles! Your pickles take straight;
All loose pickle-mixing, so menacing state,
Should sure be made treason! Then, one other thought:
Red cabbage with menace is fearfully fraught.
Disdain, curse, destroy, deprecate, hot defy it,
For it bites like small adder—leads also to riot!
'Tis impossible nearly stuff tough to digest;
In your stomach like lead such kale ruins rest.
These foregoing truths so abstruse, deep, profound,
Tonight I give to you—very clearly expound—
Remember, digest well—take into your homes;
Preserve; oft peruse in your minds, or in tomes,
For wholesome in latter they'll be found complete
Reported by Slupsky verbatim, chaste, neat,
As they fall from these lips, not coarse vitiated
By common reporters—all mangled, misstated.
But ere, men, I conclude, stern duty commands
(We ever should do, men, what duty demands),
That full warning should fall from end of this tongue
Against Argonaut—too, fellow called Young.
Disdain all advice advanced by base former;
It's always opposed me—most sound, true reformer—
Whilst that fellow Young, I'm bound, I think worse—
Damned pair put together are political curse!"
Here someone yelled "Liar!" whilst rotten eggs flew
Smash, crash, on helmet, every aim so Tell true.
Men jumped to their feet; they yelled, bellowed, howled;
Some flourished big guns; some cursed, some caved, scowled;
Good Lord only knows what had been dread finale
Had minions blue-coated not calmed weather squally.
With helmet absterged, well adjusted in place,
For Knight seldom suffered it removed from fat face,

Knight firm-voiced resumed: "I regret this affair;
It is not auspicious. Vile press may declare
My remarks were not welcome, when plainly you see
'Twas pent-up applause for great cause—too, for me.
However, hereafter, I trust you'll restrain
Your feelings slight trifle. From eggs please refrain.
Not that I'm opposed to fowl egg, understand,
Which, like standard golden, so blesses this land,
But, yet, much prefer that all here who have eggs
To offer would pass them to Abe on hall's stage
In bags, or in baskets. Men, do not with zeal,
Such ardor, dispatch them. I trust this appeal,
Which proceeds from my heart, each one here will heed.
With which explanation again we'll proceed.
What I voiced before, I'll condense, boil, repeat:
Avoid warty pickles; ne'er red cabbage eat;
Of Argonaut caitiffs make mats for your boots.
Such Thugs deserve hanging!—to be treated as brutes!
Then, argentine Young"—what Knight then meant to say
In mystery remains, for wild fight, din, debris,
Ensuing prevented supreme peroration
Knight then had in mind to grace high occasion;
For auditors raging rushed with whoop, wild hurra,
For stage as one man—for Fat Knight flew masse,
But Knight, with bold Abe, during tumult, loud roar,
Successful escaped, sliding sly out back door, [west,
Mounting bike, mounting ass, with backs turned to Gate
Fast leaving Francisco, for howling mob pressed!
But went not alone. To cheer that sad journey,
To aid, succor, save, went with them D. Kearney,
Who, up before Abe, like bright north star at night
Guided air to escape, steering safely, calm, right.
Yet was't Knight dejected. Long rode he sad, mute,
But voice at last finding thus wise talked en route:
"I most greatly regret deep truths I evoked
Such tumult, mad riot, this evening provoked.
But I am consoled. What duty said 'Do!'
I truly performed—Denis, saving, you, too!
You're brand from those burning! Great treasure I hold
More precious than richest Golcondas of gold!
Press coarse may assail, ridicule, curse, revile,
Dana's Sun do its damnedest, lash, vilify vile,
But only reply, Denis splendid, shall be,
'This my first jewel!' pointing, Denis, to thee!
You'll strengthen my cause—attract to my side,
As on through great country expounding we ride,
Great power, beauty, merit, dignity, worth,
Wealth, wisdom, renown, high respect due to birth,
Us making puissant. But, friends, let us eat.
E'en greatest reformer can't reform without meat.
Here, now we are safe from implacable foes,
Let us stop, quick dismount, regale, plan, repose."

For Knight Flew Masse.

But how, Knight, get down? E'en most ski led riders feel
It is ticklish at times to step from low wheel,
Whilst from cycle of Knight, Knight thirsting for war,
To get off, dismount, is grave problem most sore,
Sans ladder, sans derrick. But Abe, fertile wight,
Education's supporter, apt advised anxious Knight:
"There is an old adage that man must endure
Disease learned doctor cannot relieve, cure,
Which saw applies here. Being up there too far
To safely get down, you should stay where you are;
Which has plain advantage, for if you remain,
By my sister's cat's eye, 'twill save mounting again."
But Denis said, "Nonsense! No ladder we need!
'Tis naught to get down from such still-standing steed!"
Fat Knight remained mute. Said Slupsky: "I feel,
Your Highness, safe, best way 's to slide down high wheel.
'Tis attended with toil thus safe to reach ground;
Lacks dignity, too, but no one is around
To blab to reporters; likewise, you discern,
Now thus to dismount is necessity stern.
Now what's necessary I tell you, in truth,
Is respectable ever, e'en though most uncouth."
"That's true," added Denis; "whatever befalls,
We all should respond when necessity calls,
As on this occasion. His Highness can't sleep
Up there on high wheel, let alone—ahem—eat."
It put Knight to blushing that one should allude
To certain necessity polite dubbeth rude.
"But now," remarked Abe, "it may help us along
By keeping in mind how Your Highness got on
When you last mounted wheel. I joke not, nor scoff,
But take it, Your Highness, to get down, or off,
Is much easier far—is perhaps just reverse."
"When I last mounted wheel fate was so perverse,"
Fat Knight didst explain, "that I never shall know
How seat I reached. When surrounded by woe
Attended with tumult men impulsively act."
"That," Denis observed, "is a God's honest fact,
But here at this juncture reflection profound
Should logically tell how best to reach ground."
"Dead easy!" said Slupsky, with long pole supplied,
"For man down smooth sapling like this 'n' to slide,
Whilst Denis, myself, Safety steady, support,
Pole keeping in place." Coolly Knight didst retort:
"Any port in wild storm;" then he smiled saturnine
As great bulk to smooth pole he sought to confine.
Storm surely it was! Smooth pole was too light,
Or else, men, by far much too bulky Fat Knight,

For certain it is slim pole snapped in twain—
Bike, Denis, Abe, Knight, pole, all mixed in pain—
Aground in confusion, contusion, alarm.
Said Abe from debris, "It worked like a charm!
Though we all much contused, this glad fact is found:
Grave problem is solved—Fat Knight is aground;
But here now suggest, to avoid future bale,
Hereafter we ride when we can, men, on rail.
Let cattle be shipped on ahead every day,
We going in cars before making entree
Into city, or town. Thus time we shall save,
Yet making appearance both brilliant, most brave."
Fat Knight, something wroth, was disposed to berate
Abe, Denis, bike, beast—bitter curse fractious fate,
Being there 'neath mild stars, brilliants speaking of God,
Chagrined, contused, hungry, sore, sad, on hard sod.
But soon smiled Knight serene; so often dark sky
Close, sullen, terrific, in sultry July
Affrights, awes, appalls, but o'er storm, rushing rain,
Clear concave in azure, 'freshed world joys again.
So gracious Fat Knight. With jokes, jibes, humor, glee,
Repast plain, substantial, clean, abundant for three,
Knight helped prepare. After heartily eating
Together their first meal since fateful meeting,
Fat Knight sweet repose sought. Then Denis, like Abe,
Turned there in, or out. Each slept like fine babe
Quite fatigued, worn out with day's romping, wild play;
True trio were stirring before break of day,
When astounded they found Abe's ass, bite by bite,
Odd helmet of pumpkin from face of Fat Knight
Consumed had whilst Knight slept. He'd slept there so
sound,
As sweetly as seraph—aye, far more profound— [face
That munching ne'er feazed him. Now shading round
Fat Knight had mask silken of plain black in place,
But soon procured helmet, for his enterprise,
To fully succeed, not allowed human eyes
To gaze on Joved front. Hence, hero, or Knight
Of face without mask rare permitted men sight.
All neglected to pray, but sought to appease
Keen cravings of hunger by eating Abe's cheese,
Big, round shield protective valiant squire in war
Had carried in 'Frisco all wild night before,
But now immense cantle in yellow cheese ripe
Gave proof of size, sharpness of three's appetite.
Whilst brave trio regaled, fat, sterile, large ass
Packed tight in his paunch full supply of green grass,
Topped off with big thistle. "A word," said Fat Knight,
"Before we proceed. I'm convinced it's my right

All orders to issue; so now I begin:
Attention, battalion! Severe discipline
I rigid oppose, but in peace, or 'muck cess,
Fair order is vital, my troops, to success.
Sound! Sound, reveille! Wind, ye Slupsky, huge horn,
Awak'ning from slumber sloth's sluggard—young morn!
Caparison Bissile! Let's mount! Let's away!
I'll ride sterile ass whilst pair of you may
Bring careful up rear with my cycle, rich stores,
Till encounter we railway; then we'll into cars.
Don't mind my verses. Men may well oft dispense
With verses sonorous if sound is truth, sense,
In cacophonous lines. In all poesy thought
Is fat, or lean, oyster, rhyme merely shell wrought.
Attention! March forward!" As cavalcade drew
Down daisied, green slope, leaving path plain in dew,
Three broad breasts as one with ardor were thrilled,
Each with exultation expanded wide, filled.
Fat Knight rode before; never rode he in rear
Base skulker, mean coward; of no foe had he fear!
Wheeling into buff road, in splendid array,
Mars troops lusty cheered; fat ass poured loud b
Into ear of calm morning—yea, even Fat Knight
Uttered glad warwhoop, so keen fierce delight.
They martial swept on, Knight preventing all pillage;
In dim distance soon beheld troops fair village,
Which entered they boldly, Knight loud winding horn
Before only inn, which viewed they with scorn,
But, nathless, dismounted—not they, but Fat Knight.
Soon town, in disorder, to view novel sight
Rushed pell-mell mouth open, may'r pompous in van;
He bade strangers welcome, for was he kind man.
He asked them to tipple. Said, "Men, take a nip;
Then, if it be proper, discourse of your trip,
Or why thus so early, in such strange array,
You honor our town poor by coming this way."
"That gladly we will," beaming Fat Knight replied,
As stepped to pine bar, where their wants host supplied.
"But first," said Fat Knight, as he gulped ample "bowl,"
"Allow me, men, tippling to warmly extol.
It's not hard to keep sober. Your man very mean,
Flint-hearted, cold, stingy, ne'er touches poteen.
Pretenders, deceivers, also some preachers,
Full many good ladies with long-haired male creatures,
Some men, too, in Maine, with great horror, large fear,
Shun stingo, stout, brandy, gin, champagne, ale, beer,
Kimmel, blackberry, French chartreuse, sherry, rum,
Port, blackstrap, bub, vermuth, metheglin, schnapps,
mum—

All drinks nature rich with art brews, or distills,
As if drinking plenty were one crime that kills,
Whereas keeping sober is nearest approach
To virtue in many who pretentious reproach
Their peers—drunken betters! Immaculate God,
How often you see obtuse, vain, formal clod
Pompous swelling with pride that he had had spunk,
Or nerve firm, or meanness, to never get drunk!
All good men don't drink, but men wisest, great, best,
Have drunk very deep—wine often cheered, blest.
Ho, boy, fill huge flagons! Here, Ganymede, light!
Forth fetch us plenty to refresh, cheer, delight!
Come, maiden, with old wine as red as ripe lip!
As bright as thine eye! As rare, maid, as thy hip!
Come, eat, drink, be merry! Here, youth, brimming cup!
Here, Love, Health, Youth, Beauty, this Falernian sup!
Here all open hearts! Here nectar take! Glasses!
Drink deep to long life of saints, turgid asses,
Whose merit chief, best is, not that they wise think,
Greatly act, or do good, but merely don't drink!
Impartial God damn them, if e'er You damn any!
Which, Lord, if You do, You'll damn very many."
Then Fat Knight in few words his purpose explained;
Then with mayor they to breakfast. In groups remained
Awed hamlet's people in bar, inn, about,
Discussing Fat Knight, Abe, reform, Denny's snout,
Which sad night before, in camp in confusion,
When Fat Knight dismounted, had suffered contusion.
When right well refreshed, pleased trio with mayor
Strode back to pine bar, Knight calling all there
To step up in welcome. No man there refused, [used
But took each whisky straight. Said Fat Knight: "I am
So well here this morning that I feel inclined,
Considering bar stuff, with way we were dined,
To remain here all day." Town's populace cheered.
"We've had some misfortune which might be repaired;
But greater than that: Here I fain would make speech;
Great truths of reform I would have you all reach.
You men here all labor. You sweat at hard toil;
You carpenter, butcher, cultivate fruitful soil;
You do all you can, but I tell you men, pat,
Something else you must have. Alone labor's flat.
In republic like this, where all men are free,
You all will be slaves if you refuse to heed me.
Reform's now on tap. Hence"—
"I wish," said kind mayor,
"To here make apt motion: To bar let's repair.
Whilst I love reform, as I often repeat,
One thing I love more—that's good Scotch whisky neat."

All Good Men Don't Drink.

Knight's face quick was clouded; so oft August sky,
But sun hidden behind reassures watching eye
Perceiving bars argent, with gold along edge
Of mountains in heaven, bright gilding jagged ledge
In celestial range. Through black, golden-hemmed shroud
Behold azure peeping like blue eye in dun cloud!
Fat Knight some was nettled, but swallowed chagrin
Along with huge bumper of Holland's old gin,
With whisky for wash-down, marked act much admired
By village, host, mayor. Fat Knight, seeming tired,
His speech left unfinished. Village crowd went away
Whilst mayor with fine trio old sledge 'gan to play
In cool, cosy back room, where frequent coy maid
Large thirst of players to full slake essayed;
Knight drunk very deep; poured he out wisdom's store,
But growing more tired, fell flat on bare floor,
Deep sleeping stentorious. There Fat Knight so slept
Till dark-mantled evening soft, sombrely crept
Up from horizon dim—till night's children, stars,
Peeped out from blue beds. One reddest was Mars,
Earth's nearest brother, flaming rogue men abhor,
Vehement, implacable, bold wight for war.
He led twinkling host through vast sky like arched sea
Waveless, serene—fire-flecked, boundless lea!
How poor seemeth art, greatest glory of man,
When sky filled with grandeur in wonder we scan!
When sky's studded with stars in night clearest, cold,
Some orbs like to silver, some salmon, some gold!
Some still, cold, serene; some seeming to fade;
Some yellow as saffron; some peeping afraid
From out mystic distance, dazzling specks in groined sky;
Others splendidly brazen, like proud courtesan's eye!
But at last Knight, much rested, much sobered, awoke,
Rolled over, arose, yawned, stretched himself, spoke,
For tamarack calling. In bar still was mayor,
Who called up stiff drinks. Then Knight didst prepare
With Denis, bold Abe, to proceed on long way;
Knight thanked his honor, who urged Knight to stay,
But latter refused, but potent, warm, brief,
Urged mayor to join force—to become under-chief.
Full consent he glad gave, appending his name
To list of reformers. When Fat Knight saw same
He loud shouted "Hooray!" He e'en essayed jig,
For latest addition was none less than Jay Snigg!
He famous zealot who once had stirred Kansas,
But fell in disgrace—took what other man's was,
Or so posse said; hence, blanched, in hot haste he
Dug out for far West. He was dressed rather tasty,

Old, long linen duster, black frock-coat, blue vest,
White high hat, tie yellow, kip boots very best,
Red flannel shirt new, Colt's gun, cane, black bottle,
Comprising full costume. Some said he was hot hell.
Tall, thin, was he—talented. When he orated,
Which he very oft did, he great agitated
Himself, well as hearers. Once in criminal court,
He saying "Not guilty!" to some alleged tort,
He so worked 'em up they rushed in—rude seized him;
Fixed court flashed stern law, when, lo, they released him!
Much thinner than Ingalls, whom he somewhat resembled,
Jay's speaking was such when he talked thousands trembled.
He was over six feet; he resembled steel ramrod;
He weighed in good order as much as such man should;
Loud Populist true, he held that Ne-me-sis—
All other parties—was pulling to pieces
Right, liberty, justice, which, struggling, dying,
All anti-Pops were accurst crucifying.
Him Knight warm embraced; then Knight planking quarter
Bold down on bar, they all took final snorter.
Forth then they essayed; all rigged up they started,
Jay on his broncho. As they brave departed
They all shot their guns off, Jay saying, fearless,
'Twas safe so to do since town then was mayorless.
They struck out for Reed's, town not far from 'Frisco,
But north of Tilburton, thus running much risk; so
Said Mr. Snigg, knowing near frowned great prison
By felons so dreaded. Such prudence was his'n
He eschewed such resorts except on occasion,
When solicitous state would accept no evasion,
Nor smooth excuse proffered. They got into Reed's
In morning alone when wise early bird feeds.

Jay on His Broncho.

Refreshing in Reed's, they did some repairing,
But did no reforming, Fat Knight, incensed, swearing
They'd go by rail to some town for stout tent; so
Chartered fast freight for famed Sacramento.
Arriving, they fixed to assault every evil,
To most righteous end falling to like red devil.
Engaging 'lectrician, stout blacksmith, metal,
Gold, steel with copper, each man in fine fettle,
They fashioned rare helmet, three metals well beaten,
For Fat Knight in place of one ass had eaten.
Six fine incandescents surmounted new helmet,
With fluid supplied from Abe on ass well set,
Abe battery carrying, thin wires conveying
Light deadly to helmet, thus finely displaying

Large head of Fat Knight, whose fine halo of fire,
Like holy saint's nimbus, made many admire
As Fat Knight in van led bright, grand cavalcade
When through certain towns went they brave in parade.
Nor banners neglected. Jay Snigg on white cotton
In bright yellow painted, "Reform, Oh, Ye Rotten!"
"Hard Labor Is Hurtful!" "All Life Is but Breath!"
"Give Us Eugene Debs, Or, Ye Fiends, Give Us Death!"
"Jesus Christ was a Tramp!" "Men Who Toil are but
Slaves!"
"All Rich Men are Rascals!" "Lord, Cast Out Damned
Knaves!"
"Possession's Pernicious!" "All Things for All Men!" –
"One's Wealth is Some's Woe!" "But Scum's Upper-Ten!"
"True Freedom Is Lawless!" "Each Man's but Same Clay!"
"It's More Noble to Steal Than Slave Day by Day!"
Also in procession, Snigg holding work up,
Appeared banner bearing limned-to-life Magic Scup,
Atlantic-coast fish bright silver in sunlight,
But blackish-banded when dead, or in dun night.
Bold on each side of silk was emblem depicted
As natural as e'er before Knight evicted
Magic model from liquid in which Scup disported,
Fought with fin fellows, fish females free courted.
When taken from water, Fat Knight was astounded,
Thunderstruck, rattled—indeed, quite confounded,
Detecting in Scup near fin prickly, dorsal,
Two letters, T T, that on Knight with force fell,
He seeing clearly, as saw once king "mene,"
That very likely he'd yet high supreme be,
He arguing rightly, being Knight of discernment,
That T T hadst always naught but Third Term meant.
Scup highly prizing, Fat Knight had sent trophy
To Gotham for safety. Indignant, wroth he
When full informed that, by some collusion,
Dave Hill had Scup Magic. Hell, dire confusion,
Perplexity, turmoil, tumult, shame, chaos,
Distraction, ensued. Fat Knight swore that day as
Ne'er blasphemed before. That day in hot fury
He planned, plotted war whose hist'ry'll endure we
Opine through all ages, men seldom forgetting
Contests made heroic through ample blood-letting. [ing,
Refreshed, repaired, hopeful, Knight yellow horn sound-
Into great city dashed Knight with aids bounding,
Knight leading, proud blazing, exciting commotion.
It was stately sight! Surpassed e'en dark ocean
Lord Byron extolled so when he was dejected—
When he, ten to one, had brown liver affected.

His Invincible Incandescence.

Through principal street, great crowds in it staring,
Knight, Abe, Denis, Snigg, on cattle went tearing,
Knight sounding long horn, Abe mad clashing cymbals,
Kearney hard pounding drum, Snigg singing hymnals.
Thus vast throng collected outside of great city,
Where Knight essayed speech, beginning: "I pity
That person, or people, that class, or station,
In Europe, Asia, Japan, or this nation,
Reform holding light. List, friends! What I utter
Is raped country's meat, white bread, country butter!
Life-blood of republic! Bone, semen, sinew!
My word to you what to black bass fat minnow!
I bring you wisdom! I come here with manna!"
Yelled ribald newsboy, "What's the matter with Hannah?"
Knight self-possessed thus: "It's not my intention
To stir up your passions, exciting contention,
Bat stop here en route in remarkable town"—
(Loud, hearty cheers)—"on some evils to frown,
Suggesting reforms. Fellow citizens, friends:
This trip I am making to advance country's ends.
But another thing, friends: I stoutly maintain
These United States is, though in Dan's speech to Hayne
Bold Daniel declared these United States are.
I maintain Dan is wrong, though Olney, bright star!
Like Clay, noted Webster, whom I hold puerile,
Dogmatic adheres to treason-like plural.
But not to split hairs am I now before you;
Nor, friends, do I come for fault e'er to score you,
But beg your support to recover great treasure
Holds foe most malignant. With him I'd measure
Keen swords, sythes, long pikes, spears, axes, huge
truncheons,
Fight him with hard gloves on water, or puncheons,
Or even with razors, but he is base coward
As now, public, I brand him! Never brave Howard
More anxious for combat than I this minute,
But skulks, hides, craven foe! For fight isn't in it
Except with foul mouth! He, too, has rank heelers,
Boodlers, Thugs, convicts, assassins, low peelers,
Who assist, foul abet his fell, awful crimes
Disgracing this nation—so staining these times!
He base caitiff damned who holds now illegal
Scup Magic that I from deep didst inveigle—
Now own in fee simple! To push fond reform
That I have projected—to make it conform
To dictates of justice—I must full regain
Magic Scup, or all earth in woe must remain.

A Caitiff.

Without Magic Scup I am weak—I am frail;
If it's not restored all my plans great must fail.
So now I come mainly to crave your support
In war soon to open to redress foulest tort
E'er earth yet defiled! I come to implore
You men to go with me to most righteous war.
This state's one of glory! But lend me your will,
Your aid, arms, your strength, she shall wax grander still!"
Loud, long, wild applause, yet but one whiskered wight
To list 'neath Knight's banner stepped up for to fight.
That great, valiant soul, as good as armed host,
Was none other, men, than renowned beerish Most.
Him Fat Knight embraced, whilst crowd acclaimed, cheers
Succeeding appeal for "Three rousing beers!"
Some vile wag proposed. At most sad, solemn time
You'll find in this world oft despicable slime,
In census called men, who sneer, jeer, insult.
Bold enlistment of Herr caused Knight to exult;
Keg of nails, too, to open when back to freight car [star
They had slow made their way. Ere morning's bright
Appeared in wan East Fat Knight with true men
Had left Sacramento. Through woodlands, vales, glen,
They reached Carson City. Hot sun being down,
Knight's helmet ablaze, through main street of town
Marched, commotion creating. So much so, police
Apprehended paraders, giving each cell apiece.
Knight Billy-be-damned them, whilst Snigg, Kearney, Abe,
With Most, high in concert in horrid tirade
Red vengeance demanded. Each blasphemous yell
Was made most emphatic by kicking barred cell, [ing;
Pounding bars with clenched fists, great iron doors shak-
Like hyenas howling, cell furniture breaking.
When highest was orgy, when yells fell, loud rose on
Night air, authorities ordered big hose on.
When Most heard said order he dropped to cell floor.
Heard he not one word when asked, "Wha'd you yell for?"
But seemed as corse cold, but when they threw water
There into Herr's face he flew up, raved hotter
Than ere fell in faint. Full then they brass nozzle
Shove into Herr's face; letting fly, they soak, sozzle,
Gambrinus disciple. Thus at last didst subdue him.
Next morning in court to hear—to review them—
Grave judge them arraigned. Stood they in sad row
Before high tribunal. "You are charged, records show,"
Solemn court said, ahemming, "with disturbing calm peace.
How here do you plead?"
"It's a damned lie! Police"—

A Victim of Plutocracy.

So started in Herr, but rude wretch clothed in law
Drew off, giving Herr such sound swipe on square jaw
He flew crash through court window, near which Herr
stood,
Far landing below with dull, sickening thud,
Sash taking out with him, but leaving some fragments,
As sailed he through, of water-soaked garments.
Hurried forth minions six, each Irishman honest,
To Herr get, assuage, but Herr he was non est,
As they all declared when back soon, in wonder,
They reported escape. Grave court black as thunder
Cloud in July said, "He's made for tall timber, [winder!
But you, sargent, who slugged 'im, must pay for that
You should I fine, too, but this city'll manage
To find you excuse if you'll pay that damage.
But these other tramps here, especial this fat 'n',
It seems to me law says clear should be sat on.
They say they're reformers, but by their looks—manners—
It's court's honest belief they're nothing but canners.
They come in a freight; there're facts, too, revealing
That ten to one they have been hosses stealing.
But proof's not complete, so now if they'll travel,
I'll here discharge 'em, saying go to hell's devil!"
Knight's bosom heaved high, but face, behind shield,
What passions showed were not there revealed.
Discharged by gruff court, accused with effects
Made all haste for their freight, quick leaving by next
Mixed train for Reno, wherein they found Most;
Him took they on board, then turned toward east coast,
Fast passing through Vista, Hafed, Clark's, Wadsworth,
Thistle, Ryepatch, Winnemucca, Deeth, soforth,
In Salt Lake arriving. There, 'bout '47,
So didst Brigham Young, maintaining that heaven
Men certain may reach by free taking, not vows,
But stout, lusty women, sealed to them, as fraus.
Brig practiced as preached, behind leaving brood,
Live proof he for glory did all prophet could.
There Fat Knight well prospered, but not by fond plan
Czar Brigham projected to sanctify man. [store
Young thought wives so good, them oft took till sweet
Footed up, so they tell, nineteen, or full score.
Yet lived till fair age, plain proof Brigham eager
To accumulate wives, had uncommon vigor,
Or must have abstained like saints who keep Lent.
Now, there in Salt Lake, where polygamy's spent,
Fat Knight with four chiefs sallied out as before
In Carson, or elsewhere, to drum troops for war

The Reign of Law.

Magic Scup to recover from dastardly thief
On Manhattan isle. Knight declaimed rather brief
To Mormons, Jews, Gentiles, to whom near Zion
His voice lifted up. Said he: "I rely on
My just, righteous cause; men's honor, firm muscle,
Respect for plain right, true valor, in tussle—
Most dire conflict I have planned soon to wage
In Empire state. There we expect to engage
Not only arch foe, but all fiends who incline
To aid, abet, succor, damned monster condign!
I need not to tell, for think you have guessed, know,
Full cause of planned war from my manifesto,
Which months ago issued. I come here appealing
In name of reform, in truth, in fair dealing,
In name of fair justice, in name of nation,
For aid—for arms—troops. I ask no ovation;
No applause; no rewards; no trophies—delights—
But come, honest Knight, to appeal for plain rights!
But will grant returns! To far East with me toil,
Then, when we succeed, all your own richest spoil!
I ask but Scup Magic! Fine silver, gems, gold,
Which base tyrant hath, you may have, men, to hold,
Invest, use, hoard, waste. If all troops I expect
Enlist 'neath my banner, I then can effect
Reforms now undreamed! This land like lush rose
Shall blossom, be fruitful; be feared by all foes!
By all patriots loved! Then, men, not e'en clod'll
Be found but others will hold it best model!
But one other point: Those who join—go along—
Like all bent on blood, vent their feelings in song.
Notes martial thrill brave hearts—great souls flame with zeal;
Shrill, loud clarion blasts, drum beats, fifes, appeal
To men more than speeches, though latter were heard
From lips e'en of Henry, Fox, Burke, or superb
Bald-headed agnostic. But, perhaps, I bewilder;
My aim is chaste verses of great, grandest Gilder
To here recommend. If you, men, would have songs
To sing on long way as we go in great throngs,
Procure those of Watson! He loveth soft vowels;
He is clear, polished, clean—full chaste as Howells.
'Tis held, too, by gods great Wat's work is grander,
Yea, even sweeter than best thrills of Brander.
Hence, Wat recommend. I believe I may say
One song of his warbled when we martial array,
When stand fronting foe, would such vast dread inspire
They'd take to deep woods! Watson's songs, men, breathe fire!
They kindle hot passions, not passions of lust,
But valor, integrity, honesty, trust!

Brander.

Song Breathing Fire.

Now, men, in conclusion. Mormon, Gentile, Greek, Jew—
I appeal to you all! To all 'neath God's blue,
Wide, star-spangled mantle high heavens unroll
In glory, in grandeur, from pole far to pole!
Come, heroes! Take part in deeds certain to lume
Your names whilst you live—ever honor your tomb!
Deeds sure to make privates, though in fight but hour,
Higher than Cæsar, Lee, Corsican, tower!
Each one live immortal! Never-ending revered
Because with Fat Knight in war righteous appeared!"

Address quite effective, with loud acclaim hail
One thousand souls knit for weal or black bale
To Fat Knight, Scup, reform. With cressets, trump, drum,
Snorting steeds, cannon, hogs, stores, strumpets, some
rum,
Marched troops, Knight, in van, ablaze, grand, terrific,
From Zion through city to Union Pacific
Depot, cars, railway, where squadrons took cars an'
Soon shot along for dark Eastern horizon.
Speed lightning they made, suggesting mad fashion
In Dana's Sun told, when good Webb had dash on
Fleet two fifty-five, that engine made famous
Through panting to Chauncey with "nighties"—pajamas,
Or paj-a-mas, as sweet, rare bard with Dana
Called "precious load." Despite drizzling rain, a
Dark, dismal sky now, chill wind, all brave soldiers,
Like Cromwell's troopers, drew cheers from beholders
Standing 'bout stations as Fat Knight's train flew in—
At length monster train to Denver town drew in
Short time before sunup. Troops chuck took in quarters
Outside of town, where were quizzed by reporters,
Among them Tom Mosier, who from Fat Knight drew
'Steen columns, so some said, giving most bright view
Of project, war, hopes. All those who remember—
But who could forget!—say 'twas great day for Denver,
Knight's speech being chief. Surrounded by warriors,
Aldermen, mayor, policemen, pomp, lawyers,
Bands brass, martial, string, Fat Knight started speaking:
"My Troops, Fellowmen: Thus far, succor seeking,
I have come; I have seen; I signally flourish;
Not in myself, but cause noble we cherish!
Our thralldom you know. Men, I think, too, you feel
Warm ardor now thrilling these troops brave with zeal
To leave kindred, hopes, homes, babes, sweethearts, wives,
To sacrifice, mayhap, in righteous cause lives!
But what man so dastard from war to refrain
When cold tyrants attempt to force, fetter, chain!

Ovation in Denver.

None such defiles Denver!" Applause to arched skies
With hats, bottles, canes, many other things, flies.
"Nor in Colorado!" Tradition shall tell
For ages to come of long-prolonged yell
That climax evoked: how, too, with their cheers
Wild populace mingled "You bet!"—happy tears.
"But, heroes, be calm. If plain speech so astounds,
Excites, may I dare expose Cæsar's wounds?
To e'er show loved emblem—this banner hold up—
Displaying to all moving portrait of Scup
Damned dastard purloined?" Here picture of same
Fat Knight waved on high. Instanter acclaim
Like that for Plumed Knight when black Logan's boys
Blaine made victorious—gave him Illinois—
Arose, startled Denver. Fat Knight tried in vain
Mob's ardor to quell. He again, yet again,
Essayed to orate, but mob, howling hell,
Grew wilder, yelled louder, but finally fell
Into calm through exhaustion. Then placid Fat Knight
Called, "Come, all ye heroes! Enlist for great fight!"
One thousand responded. Being raw, troops so new,
With Jay them commanding, much noise, time, ado,
Attended embarking. At last safe in cars,
Three trains pull for Kansas, each stout son of Mars
Large, tin, rampant Scup proudly bearing on breast.
Till reaching Topeka, Pop hotbed out West,
At stations ne'er stopped, excepting for water,
More coal, whisky, wood, or boxes redhot, or
To take up fresh troops, who at small stations
Flagged trains to join, or make Knight ovations.
Pop state, that jakes foulest, where joint poison flows,
Makes man in moon fickle hold tightly keen nose
When passing on o'er her. That's true; you may go
Dead broke on assertion—George Ant'ny says so.
There stood from Wamego fat Rogers to buy
Fat Knight to display, or to purchase to try,
For Rogers unique would buy globe, corner air,
If God would consent—tried to purchase World's fair!
Topeka Pops cheering, Fat Knight smiling, gracious,
Some few minutes spoke, swearing Hill, most mendacious,
Should thrill them to arm—should excite them to pour
On East in great flood to wage most worthy war.
Whilst thus stood appealing, like Ware scorning peace,
Behold, there before them, renowned Libby Lease!
Said she to Fat Knight: "It fills—thrills me with fire
I long thought defunct, to see you, grave sire.

One Effect of Eloquence.

Lease always was lacking, but you—heart be still!—
So learned, ripe, large, most completely fill bill.
How this looks I know. Know I, too, servile race,
Men called, hath trampled, denied—would debase
Weak women lone, poor—down to hell wouldst us shove
For open declaring true heart's pregnant love!
But scorn I such caitiffs! Despise, deep detest,
He tyrants delighting with infinite zest
To mount—to ride o'er us! What's sauce for gray goose
Is sauce for gray gander. Whilst latter is loose
Respect cares but little, or slightly complains,
Whilst if one of us fall, great God, how it stains!
We sport then of men! My sex's deep rancor!
Mayhap parent-cursed! No hand, spar, drift, anchor!
Men swear that is just. I swear they are liars!
We're same body—flesh, blood—hot passions, desires!
Tell me trusting maiden who worships, adores,
Bold youth who seduces her, should chamber with whores
Outcast, scorned, traduced, whilst he, saying, 'God,
Repent I—forgive!'—it is just to applaud!
'Tis false, Knight, as Tophet!"

Wants One Social Standard.

"I think," said Fat Knight,
"You're practic'ly wrong, whilst the'retic'ly right.
At least, Lease, I am sure with this you'll agree:
Health mortal is hurt by promiscuity,
Especially woman's. She, Lease, is God's flower
From paradise sent to adorn social bower.
Home, marriage, maternity, to her, Lease, belong—
She sent to make life for man long, sweetest song!
Can she, Lease, do that with black spot on her name?
I ask, Lease, in candor; reply, Lease, in same,
As in public speech."

"You most prejudiced speak.
Knight's high province once was defense of us, weak
In times past declared. But now, by all gods,
From men ask we little, or very few, odds.
But, Knight, do demand, in speech, justice, clear right,
But one social standard. For that we shall fight
Till victory comes! Think, you, we should truckle,
Low bow down, cringe, beg, because, Knight, we suckle
Babes, love's sweetest proof! Ere long, Knight, I wot all
Women their babes will bring up on glass bottle,
Which men, Knight, are fitted now quite well as we
To do in broad land of brave, gallant, rich, free!
But enough of this war. I come here to dare
My feelings—say failings—to frankly declare.

I weep, pray, for all earth. Like you, I would save
This world from collapse—from becoming serf—slave!
But talk methinks vain. To bring right—fruitful peace—
I speak very boldly—Fat Knight with Bess Lease
Shouldst his fortune unite, his hopes, his heart, hands,
His aims, his endeavors, to reform all slaved lands."
Fat Knight: "Lease, your frankness doth largely atone
For suggestion unworthy—e'en dangerous—I own.
We must not thus confer."
"Is country not free
"To do what is right, Lease!"
"Fat Knight, you wrong me!
What's essential to save can never be wrong!
That, Knight, is Lease creed; that, too, be my song!
Apart we are weak, at least not so potent,
Stalwart, firm, robust, puissant, stout, ponent,
As if close, true united. Knit union of hearts
Intensifies strength of pair's projects, plans, parts,
Making us like to gods!"
"You make these cheeks flush.
Colonel Lease, please forbear!"
"You observe I don't blush!
Plan based on reform is ne'er shaded with shame!
For good e'en adult'ry adorns fairest name!
What churches call crime may oft prove brightest gem,
When need is essential, in Pop diadem!
Knight, look you to war! Dread, legalized flood
Of want, rapine, havoc, rape, murder, woe, blood!
But men call such glory! Exult as sublime,
In epic, brass, marble, colossal, curst crime!
Whilst me they'd contemn if suggest just, or hope,
For good of all men—all this earth—we elope!
Is that wisdom—justice?"
"I've heard," said Fat Knight,
"Dread war's ever greatest, highest trial of right."
"And I," said keen colonel, "have heard fools declare
This globe is not round, but an absolute square.
What we hear's often dross; what know is pure gold.
But now to first charge. Think me not over-bold,
For, Knight, zeal makes me speak—plead here on my knee—
That you cleave to my cause—cleave, too, unto me!
Thus only can nation be saved from this hour
From corporate trust—from base moneyed power!
Then, Knight, O, refuse not! But come to these arms,
Though youngest not now—not alluring in charms—

A Silent Appeal.

But strong to entwine, Knight! Strong, eager to share
Some part of vast burden so manful you bear
For weal of great nation."
"I regret, Colonel Lease,
I cannot consent."
"Then you hear me, Obese!
I'll wire my husband! I'll declare all! Then he
Wilt avenge with hard fists foul wrong you've done me,
Or pistol you proper! I'll affirm how you sought
To vilely seduce me! Ah, little I thought
You villain you are!
"Hold, female! You're mad!
I try to seduce you! I once was called bad,
But, by all ancient gods, if you I'd seduce
For silver, gems, gold, for Gentiles, rich Jews,
Then let me be damned!"
"You infernal, fat wretch!
Base scoundrel more knavish than ever Jack Ketch!
Defiler of women! Of virgins fell scourge!
You another base Burr uncastrate at large!"
So fierce she declaimed she Fat Knight much fired;
He noted her pluck—her high spirit admired.
Then he said: "Colonel Lease, words uttered in heat
Much now I regret. I regret, I repeat,
Whilst apology offer. Likewise, I implore
Your aid in reform—in this most righteous war."
"I'm yours!" loud she yelled as entered Knight's car,
Thenceforth till her death Knight's resplendent north star.
Some soldiers protested. They swore she'd abused
Man, lord of creation; had him mean contused,
Declaring him hump-backed, round-shouldered, knock-kneed,
Lantern-jawed, hairless, weak, toothless—indeed,
Mosquito-legged creature without any sense;
"But Ellen," said they, "there are men still immense.
There are Samsons unshorn, as Memphis Appeal
In Tennessee found, who fine vigor reveal
When they walk, when they sit, when lie, when they stoop;
Sweet Ellen, you wrong them. Bess, there's sturdy troop
Tall, clean, straight as pines, thick-legged, sound, lusty
In sinew—their stalwart, firm-kidneyed, robusty;
So, colonel, pine not. You've been fooled by rumors;
El, spit on your hands; take a hitch in your bloomers;
Keen keep your eye peeled, then you may discover
Male fit for service as reformer, Pop lover;
But, colonel, if not, there are still sons of Vulcan—
Cabiri—so, Lease, you need not to sulk on."

Conceived by Colonel Lease.

In Knight's car, where Lease, wast no light—no candle—
Hence, soldiers, damn 'em, laughing spun scandal,
When it is plain truth, than Euclid is surer,
Keen colonel than ice or snow is far purer.
When leaving Topeka they joined in glad psalm all;
Glad psalm, some declared, they had from Cap Campbell,
Who's Pop to backbone; who, also, deep thinkin',
Concludes too much credit some men give to Lincoln.
But leaving Topeka, Joe Hudson, Cap, trains
Shot eastward, fast flying o'er mortgaged farms, plains,
Till struck Kansas City, where gallant Warder
"The Ladies" as toast finds ever in order;
Where thrives Ryan Walker, sketch artist; where's found,
Where hopes high, Bill Warner, skilled lawyer profound;
Where hustles Abell; where, too, Colonel Gaston
Full many men hope forever could last on—
George Gaston, suave sage, esteemed missionary
In journalist field, in world literary; [losopher
Warm friend of 'Gene Field. George quaint, wise phi-
As wight, Butler paints, who read astute "Ross over."
There Horns, rare disciples of Franklin's wise art;
Star Nelson hurraing with all energy—heart; [as
Where Knight talked with Tarsney—to whom said adieu
Each engine shrieked, pulling out for St. Louis.
Proceeding said Lease: "In royal production,
Knight, busiest factor is regal seduction; [Jack,
At these Marlboroughs look! Through Belle bawd, bold
Behold lordly titles! In truth, a fine pack!
No wonder Charles Dickens was free to declare
To be of plain commons is noble. I swear
Almost to observe, Knight, how anxious our girls
To capture dukes, baronets, marquises, earls!
Then think of divorces! Land sakes, Knight, alive!
It's hardly worth while now to husband or wive.
Now marriage so failing, 'twould seem there is force
In remark that successful is average divorce.
If doubtful remain, more divorce wisdom seek,
To Hilliard, ex-Chanler, Bernhardt, Corbett, speak,
Or see Minnie Palmer, singed Langtry, fair Russell,
Loie, Bettina, bold Busby, or hustle
To jolly Abe Hummell, or Maggie Mitchell,
Or Nat Goodwin even. They facts very rich'll
Supply on demand, for they've tackled Hymen;
Each found union irksome. Oft when you tie man
To woman, though angel, knot makes confusion—
Soon damns all delight by displaying delusion."

Bill Warner.

Col. George Gaston.

Marlborough.

Ex Chanler.

So rattled Lease on with scandal, trash, chatter,
Till into St. Lou puffed three trains with clatter.
There many joined force. but certain most splendid
Queen Lil with brown troupe was. Knight her had defended
When others proved craven. No wonder then frantic
Lil rushed to Fat Knight, him hugging gigantic.
She cried "Aloha!" "Aoi!" she glad cried, too; [too.
She wept in Knight's bosom. Fat Knight deeply sighed,
Around Knight's large body, intuitive known,
Her Majesty's arms in abandon she'd thrown,
Lease jealous observing. Knight, eyes streaming, pressed
Arms strong around Lily, breast heaving to breast!
Thus mute for some time stood. Then Lease: "Such display
Becometh no Knight! I command! Break away!"
Knight, frowning, obeyed, but ere he dismissed,
Or turned from, swart queen, chaste, heartily kissed
Her left sable cheek thrice. Long, loud, mighty yell
Ascended, whilst whistles, great guns, every bell,
Joined in glad acclaim, in eyra of night
All pouring in tumult seditious delight.

She Cried "Aloha!

Lil's troupe, even thousand, each bronze-brown in hue,
Each plump as mango, graceful each as bamboo;
Gold, glossy, bronze Junos from land ever blest
With kalo, hibiscus—where cocktails are best;
From earth's Cinderella, where poi, love, mirth;
Where ginger, Jap lilies, perfume coral hearth;
Where centipedes crawl; where mad scorpions sting;
Where tinkle guitars; where in groves minas sing;
Where life is languid; where tranquil is lying
In summer eternal rare land fructifying;
Land lonesome, yet lovely! Land so Edenesque!
Where poverty's pleasure almost, so grotesque
All attempts made to toil. Rare island whose hem,
Whose garniture, sun, make isle tropical gem!
From such land Lil's warriors, not overly dressed,
Displaying much leg trim; arms bare, also breast,
High pleasing St. Louis, where crazed, common whore
Shot Morrissey honored whilst honored tough's snore
From bawd's bed resounded. He, senate's disgrace,
Was taken so swift he died stained without grace
Pious priest consecrate to grant is implored
To save Thugs from hell—to lustrate for blest Lord.
Fat Knight made no speech, but Lease wagged her tongue,
On sort of motion perpetual loose hung,
She half hour talking. She'd been talking, too, still
Had not engineers given many toots shrill,

Joined in Glad Acclaim.

Pulling out for Æolia, picking up along way
Some carloads of heroes to join in fell fray.
Chicago warm welcome extended, Swift, mayor,
Proclaiming town's greatness; speaking much of late fair;
About "Bath House John," too; of State Street Van Pragg;
How Gothamites ever in enterprise lag;
Of Field—gone, alas! Of one Luther Laf Mills,
With fine songs Italian Laf oftentimes trills;
About Hesing's lilacs; of Kohlsaat's prime buns;
Hotel Auditorium that weighs many tons;
Of William Penn Nixon; of Joseph Medill;
Of Seymour successful; of Pollasky's skill;
Great Moses P. Handy; of Victor F. Lawson;
Of dozens of others, with Journal's man Slason;
Inviting troops final to come out to lunch,
Admire lake front some, cable-ride, take some punch.
Queen Lil made reply, which Fat Knight rendered free,
Thanking Swift very warm for lunch, welcome, spree.
Then "rushed forth them troops," as papers reported;
Troops cheered, tackled free lunch, made merry, cavorted.
Fat Knight on high wheel, with brave Slupsky behind,
Led that cavalcade, which men say outshined
Anything at World's fair. Reader, no higher praise
Than that in Porkalia now can anything raise.
That's eulogy's acme—superlative, best—
Mid., fair, fixing standard all turn to as test.
Pulling out with eclat, they went at great rate
Through Harrison's town, if not Harrison's state.
As sped through Ohio, Mucklane, of Enquire
(So Town Topics calls him), Forest City Fred Beyer,
With Morrow, John Burke, space writers, reporters,
Plugs, paper liars, truth's agile distorters,
In special trains followed, Gath setting hot pace,
With Akron, Columbus, Youngstown, too, in chase.
Gath dictated rapid to troupes of typewriters,
Stenographers, phonographs, 'phones, fast inditers
Of every description, hot flashing by wire,
Express, freight, balloon, pigeons, fleet flyer,
Square acres of detail. Mucklane said he reckoned
They'd need nothing more than one special each second;
But Joe's Gotham World, far more enterprising,
Appeared, tumefactive, far more surprising,
Working four hundred presses on specials pursuing
Fat Knight, fully telling just what he was doing,
Sheets sowing en route as onward trains whirled;
When it comes to scooping it's certain Joe's World
Beats easy all hell. With Gath, Burton noted
For being to Cody, Dan Rice, deep devoted,
For Rice Burton ran with hurrah, trumpet's blare,
Brass bands, banners, so on, for president's chair.
So sped they all on—Gath, specials, inditers—
At last reaching field where Hill with fierce fighters,

Chicago Mayor Swift.

Ten thousand men bold, with Scup thief at their head,
In martial array, stern, defiant, grim, dread.
Knight's troops in same number as valiant appear
With stinkpot, club, sword, hatchet, dart, truncheon,
spear.
Flat, smooth field of battle, one side kissing wave,
Stretched oblong, suggesting in shape sombre grave,
For thousands that day proving gory to be;
Battalions, long field, main—deep, dark, sullen sea—
Not far from Gotham. Along west side of field
Stands high rugged hill, which to hosts plain revealed
Aceldama, main, troops, these latter below
In basin, affording safe, unsurpassed show
For hosts there looking down, or in from calm sea,
Expectant, excited—some sad, some in glee.
By Hill blazed D'Ana. Knight's bitterest foes
Marked spectacled chieftain. From them acclaim rose
When Charles poised mighty pen horizontal to show,
Looking Hill in grim face, approach of damned foe.
As pointed D'Ana he smiled, lips in scorn,
Specs truculent flashing! He seemed fury born
To wipe out in blood—to force into dark main—
Armed thousands Fat Knight mustered mighty on plain
As troops form in long lines, in squares, for reserve,
Let's turn for one moment to some who observe
From high hill's rugged brow. There vast, eager throng,
Impatient for action for miles stretched along.
There young Allen Thurman, famed fine in retreat—
So splendid to lead Buckeye Dems to defeat;
Tom Johnson, of Cleveland, that practical Pop,
Single-taxer, free-trader, on hill's very top;
There Divver, grand jurist, with but one defect—
Whose face, said bright Sun, doth command deep respect;
There frangible Reid with those lilacs he grew
As Cairo, old Egypt, Algiers, toiled he through;
There stood from Ohio Nash, Nevins, Hoyt, Poe,
Cox, Harris, Jones, Bushnell, old Long John also,
With Barger, with Keifer—with Locke, too, of Blade
Sat hard on in Springfield; John Clarke who once made
Speech naming great Thoman, whose picture you've seen
If closely you've read each loose, late magazine—
Thoman now in Chicago where cops on their beat
Are held up—where aldermen sell very cheap;
There Atchison Ingalls domestic, thin, bright,
Dishonest, brilliant; Troy Cy Leland so slight—
Not able, but shrewd, who prized object to win
Wouldst e'en sacrifice God, state, nation, close kin;
Morrill, banker of Kansas, who'll promise all day,
Each pledge but to break—each promise betray;
There Sunflower Scott, who some swear doth sully
Name honored, so great as that of Rome's Tully;

Drinking to Dana's Sun.

Tom Johnson.

Joe Low, second Scott; Bent, also Marsh, Murdock;
There Calvin Hood, too, of whom you have heard talk,
For once was Plumb's partner—Cal may when in coffin
Keep running for office, he's run here so often;
There Anthony, George T.; his Leavenworth cousin,
Like hell mutual hating; there even dozen
Goo Goos beside Alger, himself e'er sunning
In borrowed glory—for pres'dent e'er gunning;
Plug Tobacco Paul Sorg, made wealthy getting
Into fat office—through men amber spitting;
There chaste Jack Milholland, who, with Jennie G.,
Opposing Yvette held by Reid rather free,
Doth chaperon Virtue, Miss Gilder's chief charm,
She e'en viewing midwives with wrathful alarm.
With Jack linked with Jennie assailing vice—wrong—
Sin, high Heaven bless them, can't prosper here long.
There Mrs. "Jack" Gardner, whose gown showed deep V
Behind, whilst in front displayed tempting C;
There Thug Murphy, fireman, who brutally smote
Kilkenny Kean Corbett, whose fame's rare capote
Enveloping all earth. Base Thug, tyrant coarse,
Defenseless Kean pasted without least remorse!
But Thug much may regret vile blows, for bold troupe
Of Corbett's brave friends may immerse in hot soup
Low, insolent bruiser so base, deep defiled,
To smite Corbett weak, who'd retreat from wroth child.
There classic Mabie, whose Italian, Scotch, Greek,
Are equaled by nothing unless by Mabe's cheek;
There Hamlin Garland, marvel grandest of God,
With "collection of cowlicks" composing vast wad
Of voluminous hair deep-rooted in brain
More noted than Bacon's. There "War Is Kind" Crane,
Whose versified splendor, in capitals, trope,
Fulfills—yea, surpasses—highest yearnings of hope.
Incomparable Crane! Ear of song never heard
In Eden, high heaven, in Newburg, such bird.
Oh, Christ, what sweet music! Could Sirens hear him
Near Sylla, Aeaea, God, how they'd cheer him!
There Ducey with sermons that fully compare
With Talmage, or Dixon; there Rafferty rare
Agnomened Paresis. So distinguished, you know,
In Rome, on occasion, P. C. Scipio.
There Harlan, Judge Trimble, who bitter oppose
In marble fine female without any clothes;
There Dr. George Hepworth, whose fiction chaste, deep,
Must e'er compel nations to thrill, applaud, weep;
There Voice-Prohib Johnson, holding water so good
He'd thank God for sending one more Noah flood.
There Strohm, Morris Stevens, Ashbaugh, Preston, Grute,
Jim Runnion; Doc Edwords, who went for to shoot
With redskins out West, Doc learning to eat
With relish, great gusto, dog's well-prepared meat.

Cal Hood.

Correction of Corbett.

Frye.

Budd.

There James Gordon Bennett, who thrills waning world
From Paris, great Gotham, through pure, touching Herald;
There Alfred Austin, who would many delight,
Would taste greatly oblige, by refusing to write;
Bayed Alfred Austin, who, as each Britain knows,
Writes verses better than rough roustabout prose;
Mild Alfred Austin with adz, hatchet, plane, saw,
Turning out tuned heroics despite crim'nal law;
Stanch, true Alfred Austin, whose leaden lines bring
Regret that events still compel him to sing;
Grand Alfred Austin, whose pure, laureate verse
Unique is, unequaled, none, bards, being worse;
Transvaal Alfred Austin, whose deepest, black crime
Isn't treason, nor murder, but reeling off rhyme.
There Mrs. Van Rens'lear, Colonial Dame,
Fault finding with Franklin since he all aflame
Sought certain maiden; too, because Mrs. Van
Found Benjamin never had been jontleman.
Weep, world, for poor lady! Heave, also, sore sob
That genius wast Ben 'stead of blue-blooded snob.
There New Jersey John Griggs, Maine Frye, Cockrell, too,
With Peffer, Budd Doble, renowned Richard Blue;
There O'Connor, of Broome, one time so excited
To say Union Leaguers should be full indicted—
Might go plumb to hell, too; Rabbi Wise claiming
Oysters are kosher, wise rabbi proof naming;
Chauncey I. Filley, from 'way in Missouri,
Where some think late war still rages in fury;
Among free-silverites who'd journeyed afar,
In big, argent helmets, were Alec Del Mar,
M. Butler, Jim Perry, Omaha Ryan;
Joe Sibley declaring Carlisle had been lyin'—
Lying knowing he lied; there too, unappalled,
That great silver Samson, renowned Archibald;
Cunningham, Adams, with Fitzpatrick, mayor,
With Tennessee Harris. Othér silverites there
Were Walcott, Clarke, Eagle, New Mexico Prince,
Brown, Warner; one Jones, oft alluded to since
Mad mouthing in Memphis. Along with same crew
Were Money, one Evans, Mr. Dave Turpie, too.
Observing stood Arkell on yacht out at sea
With Hamilton sketching. William J. seems to be
Inclined to Dutch dinners, but day of damned fight
For blood he, deeds awful, had keen appetite,
Which same much appeased was. Out of New Jersey
On hand was Werks. There, too, Carl Schurz. He
Some thought was craven for refraining from fighting,
But Carl, composed, was content with sharp sighting.

There Rowdedow Grace great. Beside him fat Hackett,
Deacon, or uncle, in red Cardigan jacket.
Ep Howe with them whiskers, far famed in Candor,
Performing for Platt, said, "This'll be grand, or
I'm much mistaken." Ep often arises
When sagely observing to marvelous surprises.
Charles Thormouth O'Farrall, whose speeches rival
Those of pure Divver—are sure to survive all—
Attracted large circle by gems he didst utter
To that bird of song, sweet warbler, B. Cutter—
Bloodgood of Long Island. James Whitcomb Riley,
Harp dialect playing—sometimes that style he
Assumes with success—was joined on big banjo
By Aqua Funk, they performing fandango,
Mike Callahan, terror, exciting to dancing
As gaily as ever assemblyman prancing
In Mike's Chatham dive. There bold Barney Biglin,
With Ans G. McCook, stood watching them sig'lin'
In plain down below, whilst Lawyer Tom Bradley,
With John L. O'Brien, looked on pensive, sadly,
As if thinking of night when many regrets
O'Brienites greeted at swell Brunswick, such pets
As Hess, Goff, Tom Platt—aye, even Sloat Fassett—
Excuses submitting. But Schultz didn't pass it—
Fat banquet!—but sat at board spotting dishes
Along with Dry Dollar eating flesh, fowl, fine fishes,
As did Donohue, Goetz, McManus, one Sweeny,
Police Justice Meade, Jim O'Beirne, Jack Delaney.
Among host attracted to see those foes prod, sin,
Cut, slaughter, stab, die, wise, rare Larry Godkin,
Ex-traveler commercial. There Roger Quarles Mills,
Once likened to gopher, stood rooted. He fills
Some parts of Texas, but in Uncle Sam's eye
Is smaller than landscape delightful to spy
In mare's purple pupil. Wat Hardin was there
With sixteen to one—also look of despair.
Quite nigh unto Wat, behold renowned Teddy,
So fond of green tea, e'en black when "drawed" ready
By Executive Strong, true reformer stanch, bitter—
Streckler admirer, huge 'bacco-juice spitter
From state Buckeye called. In song, story, sequel,
History, worth, where, pray, William's equal?
Bill Edwards looked on from side of Tom Waller,
That splendid Cuckoo. Bill offered one dollar
Or two hundred thousand at odds, or even,
On Chieftain Hill, likewise on Knight Stephen.
Jim Campbell abused, then praised so, by Clarke,
Assailed keen by King—for Jim's softest mark

James and His Harp.

St. John's Successor.

Hetty.

For Buckeye satiric—stood by Boodler Brice,
Who's honest with men—pays each his set price.
Loves Sugar Trust, too, but, then, as to that,
'Tis failing, or virtue, of nigh each Democrat.
Upham, of Wisconsin, observing, alert,
Who once for Abe Lincoln removed coat, even shirt,
In White House wound showing soon after big battle,
With Joe Manley talked, remarking, "Knight's cattle'll
Put up hellish fight!" From famed bargain counter
Appeared Pious John, like Andy, mounter
From low estate high, proof goodness, prayer, barter,
May talent surpass. That true, surely martyr
Is greater than genius. Beside merchant saint
J. Foraker—Benson—so icy no taint
Should ever approach him. Pens, guiltless of harm
In hands editorial, joke of "Fire Alarm"
When Benson is broached, for Benson, like Blaine,
'Tis palpable ever has on stalwart brain
Hopes presidential. Like him—too, close by him—
Long John, of Mansfield, who, some say, 's been lyin',
Defiling, defaming, not quick, but great dead,
In tart, ponderous tome few persons have read,
Or read ever will. In true statesman it's deeds,
Not books all may write, that majority reads,
Remembers, reveres. Benton, Grant, Sherman, Blaine,
Quartette viewed with pride, applauded each name,
Why stoop to smudge inkhorn, to sore-chafing pen,
When latter all know is great tool of small men? [John
Nigh Sherman quailed Foster with Platt, whom Long
Eyed fiercely in passion, them casting upon
Cunctipotent scorn, hissing "Judas! Is-car-i-ot!"
Their ears scorching, curling, so flaming, white-hot
Breath, words, incandescent. Then "Pah!" Sherman said
As insolent passed them, majestic John's tread.
They blanched, drawing far each within screening shell
Like dog-assailed turtle, knaves saying, "John's hell!"
Tom Byrens, Lemuel Quigg, Jim Clarkson, one Collis,
Dudley, Jim Belden, Rehasher Lew Wallace,
Bliss, Root, Horace Porter, Lauterbach, Thomas,
Hiscock, Steve Elkins, Hetty Green in gray "wamus,"
Brookfield, Franc Hendricks, Port Henry Witherbee,
Ex-Consul New, quite close together. Now, either we
Saw quite indistinct, or there from Herkimer
One Warner Miller, fit man for clerk, or mayor,
Pres'dent, duke, king, czar. There, too, sat deep sighing
Aged Winter, moist bard, o'er ivy spray crying,
Tears streaming down, like big drops in tornado,
Soaking, full soiling, fine photo of Ada.
There many Detroiters, along with live set
Potato Mayor Pingree beside winsome Pet
Blue-eyed in amaze, but e'er eager to swear
Detroit blest forever through tuber-famed mayor.

There Justice Jerome, who, working for "Tiddy,"
For whusky selling sent up Irish widdy,
Jerome's proudest act. There Edward Apollo
McAlpin, much fuller of grace than swift swallow—
Beautiful, brilliant, loved idol of ladies,
Comfort of mothers all, wept for by babies.
There Tamsen, also—of sheriffs much greatest,
Most glorious, prudent. No other state hast
E'er equaled Tam., for he's sure hottest liner.
Behold there, also, Perfecto Clay Miner!
There Cissy Fitzgerald, mild, shrinking, sweet flower,
Chaste talking of dukes to Reid thin for full hour.
There Jimmy Van Alen—also, William Kissam
Vanderbilt auric; close by Arthur Grissom
Poetical, polished. There, also, from Bristol,
S. Pomeroy Colt, who may be should pistol
Great Grover's friend Van, but Colt, far more cruel,
Cold statutes, not steel, selected for duel,
But yet didn't battle. Sure his honor is slight
Who swears honor's wounded, yet for it won't fight.
There Loie Fuller; there, too, in white breeches,
In pink coat, high top-boots, that man who bewitches
Everything female—fine, picturesque Allan—
If Town Topics's true. Bryce had for stanch pal an'
Fly equal companion with him one Vingut,
Along with some hounds—also very thin slut,
For they'd been for foxes—had breakfasted at Baldpate—
With "Bud," Schenck, some others; there were to watch fate,
War, carnage, havoc. Most bland man, large, portly,
Ballingham—Brattle—serene, solid, courtly—
With Brown—Bill Lycurgus—watching stood waiting
For hell to let loose. Bill late was donating
Fine fifteen-foot fountain in speech filled with fire
To Barrington town. Near tiptop of slim spire
In bold letters enduring's philanthropist's name;
Where other such statue! Where, gods, grander fame!
There full-bearded Lexow; there blithe Russell Sage
Chipper at eighty now; Dick Kerens in blind rage
At "Apes"—anti-Papists. There, too, gabbed amain
Those e'er-talking Goo Goos in cart-tail campaign.
Among them were Lewis, Morse, Evans, Gould, Price,
Welling, Pears, Scharton—they all free with advice
Surcharged to collars. Beside pure Goo Goos
Was John Friederrich with prime lot of Garoos.
There Morton from Rhinecliff. He, though full of years,
Is not now seeking God, but phantom that cheers
Hope, high ambition, to hard struggle, scheme, lie,
To oblivious end. Why not honored die
In home quiet like Thurman? But, come to think,
E'en Old Roman braved storm. But may be to sink
Is nobler, far better, than never to sail
Disdaining lashed ocean, storm's menaces, gale.
Suave Depew—Peach Depew—smooth, taciturn man,
Beside astute Platt, was there in host's van,

Loie.

Of Rhinecliff.

Matt.

Mac

Peace Peach profound, silent. So seldom words come
From close mouth of Depew some hold him quite dumb.
Yet he one time was heard. He once proclaimed Reed,
Morton, Ben, Allison—McKinley, indeed—
Irresistible each if named to assume
Role fond expected to work Democracy's doom.
Depew's forte's not speech, but e'er greatest doth shine
When for harmony's sake invites wranglers to dine,
As lately did Peach, but since fine banquet strife,
If report tell plain truth, has been even more rife.
But Depew did his best; his courses were fine;
His smiles were then sweetest; superbest his wine;
Low music entrancing; fresh flowers most rare;
Each story bright gem. So, were malice nursed there,
Fault lies in men's hearts. Peach did all he could,
As knows Brackett Reed, or at least Thomas should.
Reed also saw fight, which close didst survey
Through field-glass him handed by Beaver Matt Quay,
Hopeful Allison near them, but it seemed to those there
That Tom, wily Platt, wished Al otherwhere.
Clean-shaven McKinley dark-browed, olive-skinned,
Fat-handed, small-footed, round, stout, double-chinned,
Blue-tinted where shaven, tawny-green forehead high,
With small, Roman nose, through keen, deep-set, dark eye,
Black slouch hat in hand, small lips firm compressed,
Intent surveyed slaughter. In black neatly dressed,
Hair straggling o'er brow, could e'er mortal suppose
McKinley with Quay, with great Blaine, with Platt, chose
To league to beat Ben, whose craft cleared their rocks—
Who got there triumphant first dump out of box?
But appearances lie so wise men seldom heed
Signs physical, facial, but judge man by deed.
Next, Harrison stood, with his forehead bulged, full,
Large head upon neck very short—so oft bull—
Skin waxy-sallow, trimmed hair nearly white,
Thin quite on top, much like McKinley in height,
Nose small, pugnacious; hair-covered full face,
Optics gray-blue. Ben in voluble race
Is peerless, superb; in his talk his voice sounds
Piccolo, pleasant. It is judged Ben in pounds
Weighs crowding two hundred. About Ben's an air
Suggesting omnivora, plantigrade bear,
But battle scene thrilling, thousands there fighting,
Screaming, beheading, to hell going, smiting,
Morose Ben delighted. As often appeared
Fine strategy, valor, loud Benjamin cheered.
There were others, kind reader. Those named very few
Assembled on hill war cursed to view.
Watching host spread for miles, whilst out on blue sea,
Calm, smooth as French mirror, gay craft countlessly
Dotted imperturbable deep. Day, battle field, clime,
United propitious to aid glory's crime.
One word more of field. 'Twas like famed one of old
Where Hannibal Romans trapped, killing them cold-

Blooded, terrific, not showing one quarter,
If Livy, who tells it, told truth as reporter.
Hill's troops seemed some strongest. He them commanded,
His chief aid D'Ana. Next ranking, demanded
Sam Beardsley attention. His eyeballs shot fire;
His elephant bulky was, too, in fine ire.
With Hill next bold Crawford, fierce Illinois son
Named after Monroe. Dogged Croker next one
In rank Hill supporting. Stout, stud-horse, cool Dick,
Tweed's greatest rival, shaggy-browed Warwick Mick,
Built like tough scrapper for arena, or ring,
Intrepidly fought. He was oft heard wild sing
War songs in Celtic as rushed dealing death;
At other times cursing, oaths clogging hot breath.
That day Dick did nobly, not fleeing as when
Under fire took passage for Britain. Few men
Behaved with more courage. Hill's foes Richard slew
Were fully one hundred—some swore even two.
Next Corrigan slender, shrewd, Middle-age cleric
American born, but oft paid panegyric
For leaning toward Rome. He makes Cath'lics feel
Within glove of velvet stiff hand of hard steel.
Delicate, undersized, as telleth Howard,
Yet firm fighter born like Hughes—never coward.
Virile he stood, holy robed, with gold casket,
Mounted with silver, so large as peck basket,
Relics containing. There he'd bones of Sts. Paul,
Dominick, Peter, de Sales, Andrew, John, all
Plain Vatican stamped. There, too, Virgin's veil
With cloak of St. Joseph—St. Francis's coat-tail;
With relics, likewise, of Augustine, of Anna,
Of Philip of Neri, but none of St. Hannah.
Along with said relics was some of St. Clair;
Piece, too, of true cross reposed potent there;
Sacred thorns from Christ's crown; small portion of sheet
His body wast wound in; large bone firm, complete,
From arm of St. Ann. He'd, too, a job lot
Mrs. Throop in her travels in Italy got
For church in New Jersey. So armed how could ill,
Woe, disaster, defeat, befall cause of Hill
Archbishop espoused? Few soldiers but pressed
Sacred relics to touch—be evermore blessed
By coming in contact with fragments there stored
From Rome, earthly home of Catholicized Lord.
There Tillman with pitchfork, from prongs of which hung
Some fæces in senate he'd dropped from glib tongue
When plastering "Judas," Kentucky's Carlisle—
When went, too, for "Tyrant" in best saloon style.
Such some of Hill's heroes. His troops there afield
Stood Germans, Poles, Dagos, Huns, Irish, revealed,
Scarce one English speaking, that deep accursed tongue
Damned menace to Erin! There Poles, Dagos, Hun,
Their countries' flags flying, disdaining poor rag
All red, white, sky blue, some revere as best flag

Corrigan.

That ever yet kissed God's sunlight, or thrilled
True men to brave deeds. Great Tammany filled
Hill's ranks nigh alone, bold, grand mass displaying
Crosses, blest, blazing candles; holy water conveying
In tubs, bottles, jugs; some, too, carried censors
Gray holy smoking, held better than Spencer's
Rifles far-famed. But it were foul libel
To say in Hill's army were book called God's Bible,
But many banners, green silk ones—some satin—
St. Patrick (with shamrocks, with Celtic, smooth Latin
Inscriptions) displaying, under Pat's feet
Dread, venomous snake. Mike, Shamus, Pat, Pete,
Each prayed to Blest Virgin; some, too, on green sod
Confessed there contrite before meek men of God
Rich surpliced in ranks to prepare warriors' souls
For glory above. But, hark! Drum heavy rolls!
Away off afar south Knight's warriors like bees
In separate squads swarming! Chiefest with these
Full-armored Fat Knight. He, in plates of thick steel
All enameled with gold, from head down to heel,
Intrepid abike, through vast, brazen trump roars
Blasts shaking firm hills. Stentorian Knight pours
Defiance profanest, shaking, flashing on high
Blade Muramasa, throwing back to blue sky
Sol's strands of bright gold. In field, fight, or hall,
Earth never had seen such Amadis de Gaul.
Just ranking below sat, collected, calm, Dan,
Keen, truculent Mars, before him mapped plan
Of field, showing troops, divisions, each chief,
Sappers, stores, arms, reserves for relief,
With banners enscupped. There next in brigade
Invincible warrior, most redoubtable Abe
Astride tawny lion Forest king's dreadful roar
Deep echoed loud, as host by sea's shore
Prepared fell to slaught. With lips curled in menace,
Blood-curdling to see, next there behold Denis
Vast ostrich atop. From waist down to knees
Concealing legs bulky hung scalps of Chinese.
There, too, Winslow Warren, arch-chief of Cuckoos,
From calm, cultured Boston, where he fills fed'ral shoes,
Collector he being, declaring Grove prize
Most excellent, precious, from God's fruitful skies,
All men surpassing—more grand, as half-Peffer one,
Than Lincoln, George, Grant, Adams, Tom Jefferson,
Winslow proud carrying, he astride whitest ass,
Scup banner, he loved so, in front martial mass,
Scup bearing T. T., that all men could discern
With ease their true meaning. He, too, had large urn
In which Winslow hoped, if captured was Scup,
To place sanctified fish—there safe lock it up.
There renowned Potsdam Sams, hell's wonder in war;
In peace, too distinguished; he prop of main corps.
Next Colonel Lease, in tin pants, or bloomers,
Cut bias behind, important with rumors,

Invocation on the Field.

War's red, lethal bruits. There Jay Snigg, in hot glow,
Mad tears field athwart, his mount high, white-as-snow
Bactrian camel. There ahorse, like Thor, god,
High flashing fell falchion, defying foes, Pod
Sat as oak rooted firm. Dread Dismuke on horse
One thing awful seemed. Herr Most, shouting hoarse
"Ein bier!" intermittent without rest or flag
Kept constantly running from abroached, sturdy keg
Three stout German serfs. Frightful Herr rode atop
Machine like beer spiggot, in stein helmet green hop.
Satolli clean-shaven in red cassock with cross
Impressive, beads counting, rode triple-crowned hoss.
Fierce, dread, by grand chief, close by Lil's troops in green,
Pure Parkhurst good, grave, so magnific, was seen.
Pouring forth from large mouth, extensively wide,
All beheld rapid flow a n'er-ending tide
Of eloquence sound. He full-armed, by fat chief,
Fist shaking at Hill, yelled loudly "Base thief!"
Who sneer'd back quick reply, he placing left thumb
To nose; then, deft making right pollex to come
To left little finger, he rapid in glee
Flirted seven slim digits. 'Twas sight good to see!
By Parkhurst loomed Botts, puissant, dread Dink;
Dome Geza next towered, in war very pink,
By Gingery close. He, each nerve straining, tugs
Shag bison to rein in. Sa-po-dilla Scruggs
By Duby Dibble, bold latter in talk
With Comstock, Pod, Koozer, Kolb, Skaggs, Coxey, Balk.
There Headsman Adlai, beside dusky queen,
With truculent blade, he Scotch-Irish spalpeen.
There also Nies Nies stout, Rhine Opitz, Punk Hone,
Lee Peak, whiskered Wash. Lil's troops stood alone
To chestnut-brown hips bare, from waists jutting out
Short skirts as in ballet. Each wore, too, coarse clout,
But slim, shapely legs nude. Each spear carried, shield.
Lil's troops most observed of all there afield.
Huge elephants, lions, rhinoceros, bear,
Giraffes, elk, bison, heroes bearing, caved there
Knight's forces among, but afoot mostly troops,
Like Amazons amber in sparse, island-made suits.
Such both sides in part. 'Twould much too long detain
In detail to depict all dotting smooth plain
By reporters surrounded. They there in platoons,
In swarms, countless numbers—above in balloons—
To photograph, sketch it, describe, to bird's-eye,
Exaggerate, bungle, to mix-it-up, lie.
This alone true report! All others offered,
Tho' written by Howard, by Gath, or vain Crawford,
Are greatly inferior, tho' more comprehensive.
Concrete truth surpasses loose detail extensive.
But this poor digression, which here, at this season,
We candid admit, is mighty nigh treason.
Now behold with us field; look down along shore;
See troops massed, divided, deploying for war!

Going Where Glory Waits!

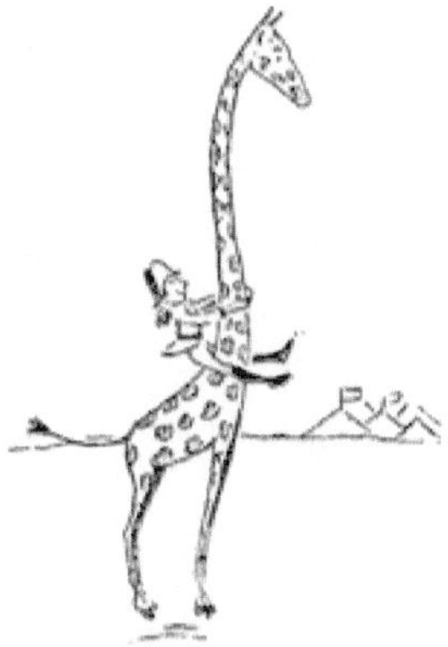

A Reconnoitre.

See, too, dashing steed! All foam! Open wide
Red nostrils distended! 'Tis Hoax! He doth ride
Like whirlwind—tornado! Impelled on by fate,
Spurs savage, deep rowels, afraid he too late
May reach Marathon. But now wet at last stands
Steed panting by Knight, who proffers both hands
To Hoax, who, dismounting, doth modestly kneel,
Clasping left leg of Knight, kissing gold-mounted steel
Whilst thrilled thousands, countless on high hill, on sea,
Tumultuous cheering! Work detained Hoax, but he
Flew, job completed, to part take in mad strife—
To yield best assistance—if need be, sweet life.
He far stronger than host, for there with him Hoax bore
Famed legal attainments—all best legal lore
He hadst easy acquired, at least largest part,
Before yet he of age, so early didst start,
As tells us himself frank in life didst prepare.
He delved very deep; with uncommon care
Read he close all decisions of high courts supreme—
Those, too, of Georgia, with text-book in between,
Ne'er waiting for causes to give hint, or cue,
But arming for all, more than Blackstones could do.
But Hoax is fine genius. His lustre bright glowed,
Whole field illuming when still stood, or fleet rode.
His weapon huge volume in iron bound, thick,
Fixed firm in cleft end of stout hickory stick.
On storied head, with legal substance full, fat,
Large, broad-brimmed, cockaded, black, soft, slouching hat,
In which were bright feathers, perhaps a full score,
Pulled out sturdy cocks that Knight's troops, bound for war,
En route, chased, caught, killed, or captured in coops,
Then scalded, well picked, gutted, fried, put in soups,
In potpies, in dumplings, or fricasseed—boiled,
Made into salads, brown roasted, or broiled.
Kill wholesale of fowls as troops flew through each state
Wast something awful, as true records relate.
Wild shrieks of fat roosters, plump hens, getting killed,
With consternation maids' simple souls filled,
Whilst all tenderest hearts, best blessings of farms,
Were shocked, fluttered, frozen with grief, pain, alarm
No cock then was safe; no Bantam, no pullet,
Nor even chick, escaped unerring bullet,
But tough old, tender young, fond mother with brood,
Were all fierce hunted down—to death done for food.
For miles balmy, blue air, when stirred by stiff breeze,
Fowl feathers full filled. Chickens, ducks, turkeys, geese,
Proud peacocks, shrill guineas, doves cooing, all fowl,
Were slaughtered, cleaned, cooked. Domestic birds' yowl,
Deep sobs, cries of grief, heard all night long, all day,
All stout, granger hearts filled sore with dismay.
Knight's army appeared as swept on, sworn foe
Of all daring to cluck, quack, hiss, gobble, crow.
So rich feathered fodder, so fowl daily fare,
All those ample feeding soon features showed rare.

.ating in Danger's Face.

For instance, Lib Lease. Upon each leg of her
There sprouted out horny, hard, sharp, savage spur.
Likewise upon Hoax—Hoax, so proud of those legs—
Whilst Olney, some wagered, laid actually eggs!
Puissant Fat Knight, who ate monstrous of duck,
Quacked oft as sound slept. Great Carlisle wast heard
cluck.
Chaste Comstock, like Parkhurst, with rancor abused,
When night spread her pinions, inclined wast to roost.
Carl Browne, Koozer, Coxey, whene'er spying hawk,
Alarmed dashed for cover—stack, coop—each asquawk.
Dome Geza'd crow lusty, whilst Dink on fence rail
Wouldst, arms frequent flapping, try flying, but fail.
Herr Most, Libby's Weaver, Dirk Balk, bloody Waite,
Web-footed grew early—waddled, too, in their gait—
Whilst sainted Satolli, from Italia we get,
With Dominis swarthy seemed certain to set.
Adlai, Scruggs, Peffer, ennobled in hair,
Loud sung guineaese, rubric combs showing rare.
Simpson, Abe, Altgeld, Warren, Sams, Parkhurst, Most,
With Pulitzer, Choey, many more in brave host,
Quacked,crowed,gabbled,gobbled; wouldst,too,often flirt
With feet whilst with noses for worms pecked in dirt.
But most of large army, regaled upon swine,
To grunt, often root, didst quite constant incline;
When along 'gaged in broils, all fours on, they'd clout,
Bite, curry, belabor, squeal lusty, use snout,
Proof potent to all that most men are in breed,
Belief, temper, so on, much moulded by feed.
But hark! Martial music! Drum, trump, clarion shrill
Loud sounding, re-echo, reverberant thrill
Armed foes, rapt spectators, yet call not to bleed
Battalions, divisions, but Fitz, Corbett, heed
Alarums of war, stepping out face to face.
From Hill's forces Bob, from Knight's Corbett. Grace
Attends every motion of Corbett as he
Confronts Kangaroo, pendant arm reaching knee.
Before serried ranks, massed, ready for war,
Vain Corbett, John's hoodoo, with huge pompadour,
But not in ring costume, as in former age
When Mace, Tommy Hyer, Sayers, Heenan, in rage
Punched, smashed, welted, gouged, fast sending in blows
Ribs breaking, teeth smashing, flat spreading pug's nose,
But there pair in dress suits, as if at swell ball;
They there not to counter, to upper-cut, maul,
But, more scientific, to smite, parry, reach,
With Smart, Webster, Worcester—with nine parts of
speech—
Match finished to fight, irrespective of rounds,
Until from one vanquished no more issue sounds.
Bob not far from Knight, whilst, most pluckily, Jim
With Parkhurst, his second, talked loudly with vim.
Parkhurst Knight selected, well knowing Park's skill.
Bob's second was Allen, whose first name is Bill.
He's famed in Nebraska—famed mostly for wind;
He once talked for hours, gyrated, yelled, dinned,
In speech long against time. Each second had rhyme,
Prose, thick, bulky volumes. Lease, fluent, kept time,

Champion Contest.

The Antique Method.

Whilst phonographs, burnished, to note every word,
Sound, syllable, whisper, mute listened. Low's heard
Each second warm coaching, Parkhurst urging Jim
To imitate Talmage, to use synonym,
To vent keen invective, to utilize boast,
Hurl satire, infamy, blot, taunt, reproach, roast.
So, somewhat, B'Llallen. His counsel to Fitz:
"Hold force in reserve. Don't draw from Greek, wits,
Rome, Latin, or classic, but steadily pour,
Whilst parrying Corbett, terms sailors, mad whore,
Pimps, roustabouts, utter. Small, hard words are best;
French, Latin, eschew, Bob, but Saxon with zest
Spit into Jim's person. Nor is it amiss,
To make 'em emphatic, to sibillant hiss.
But start calmly, easy. Perhaps for awhile,
When coming to counter, Bob, sinister smile,
For well I remember, advising you here,
No logic on earth can e'er pivot-blow sneer."
So dressed, so advised, so prepared, flowing foes
Dread stand face to face there to fluent fling prose,
Dithyrambic sallies, hot adjectives, verse,
Adverb, conjunction, hissing expletive, curse.
There fierce face to face, as when beasts savage roar,
Not fang, but stout Saxon fell weapon of war;
Jim, all men allowed, more skilled was in speech,
But Bob, all admitted, could much farther reach
For sentence, or word hard. No man was more spry—
More shifty, more tricky, with "me," "him," or "I;"
But with interjection, with adjective, verb,
Jim's foes raging, bitter, declared him superb.
In science each equal; alike'd trained severe—
Bob under Harvard, Jim Yale. Maddened cheer
Smote ambient air as they toed up to scratch
Skill, tongues, to test in what seemed equal match,
Tho' some, knowing Parkhurst, inclined unto Jim,
His ardent pluggers putting much stuff on him.
Some, too, knowing Allen, what record he'd made,
How Bob had been trained, freely many bets laid.
"Time!" called Colonel Lease. Intent, keen, upon guard,
Each opened with "Liar!" Then they gamily sparred,
Ten seconds perhaps, when hot Corbett let loose,
Quite playful it seemed, with "You swarthy pappoose!"
With "Slouch!" Robert countered, also rubbing fur
Up wrong way by smiling, "Jim Corbett, you cur!"
So round number one. In next round, second, biff
Came Corbett with "Squealer!" followed neatly with "Stiff!"
But Robert was there! He reached out with "Skin!"
Jim's only retort, "You fight most with coarse chin!"
Parkhurst loudly laughing. Then foes give, as take,
Till, mingling incessant "Dude!" "Coward!" "Chump!" "Fake!"
Gong sounding, retire, Jim deep delving in rhyme;
Bob fed upon Pulitzer till Libby called "Time!"
Scarce showing one word, or, as some said, "one blow,"
Beginning round third, Corbett loudly howled "Go!
Monkey, fight Ingalls! He's thin dub in your class!"
But Jim never feazed him, Bob hurling back "Ass!"

As fresh as dewed daisy, some doubting whether
Either could vanquish, both talking forever.
So round after round, till in round twenty-eight,
Jim made some impression, rib-roasting with "Skate!"
But Robert returned, putting in on Jim's bulk
With force most tremendous, hot-hissing out "Skulk!"
When Jim, swift retorting, attacking Bob's nut,
Sent in deft, incisive, "Abhorrent snide! Gut!"
'Twas seen foes were warming. Men, theretofore cool,
Began losing reason. Bob called Corbett "Tool!"
In round twenty-nine hot, but James merely laughed,
As smoking Sweet Cap, said he, "Kang, thou art daft!"
Then Robert to James, "You're small Pompadour pug!
Low, barn-storming swindle! No earthly-good mug!"
Allen thereupon winking, as much as to say,
"My man is improving! I've coached 'im aufait!"
But changed soon his tune, for Jim fierce retorted,
"You're hypotenus low, obtuse, base distorted!
You're hydrocephalic! You've got plumbago!
I believe, on my honor, you're a red-headed Dago!"
There ended prize contest, or high trial of skill;
All rules they disdaining, they scrap, as in mill,
Phonographs smashing over—naught showing art,
Science, fine language, but low, base, brutal part
Today's rings abhor so. Stiff contest in ring,
E'en seconds contending with jab, punches, swing,
Brought war to quick focus. As we noted before,
Massed troops stood impatient for glory, game, gore.
Now all's in commotion. Shout leaders, rolls drum;
Divisions, battalions, corps, to right-about come;
Beasts caper, wild plunging; arms rattle; foes yell—
All signs signal showing how soon martial hell
Shalt reign awful, dreadful. In no other age—
Sedan, Tours, Phillipi—hadst troops in such rage,
Such ardor, such order, so captained, appeared—
Hadst nations, all peoples, so wondered, so feared
Solicitous, heart-sick. No wonder awe thrilled
Each anxious spectator; that every heart, filled
With deepest foreboding, so palpably beat
Sounds measured suggested war charger's mailed feet
Earth smiting, or pavement, as hurtled on car
In Rome's old, palmy days, when pastime wast war.
But now mute stand thousands. With dart, bludgeon, bill,
Spear, stinkpot, sword, truncheon, most weapons that kill,
Armed there every soldier to wage lethal strife,
To decimate, mangle, take God-given life.
Now charge foes terrific like tempest of hail
When hurricane's leader grand—when victory bale.
Men, beasts, mad battalions, impetuous flew
Hamstringing, hacking, ripping-up, as they slew
Precipitate, headlong. With swords, deadly darts,
Long spears, flying engines, all war's awful arts,
Perform troops prodigious—evicerate, kill;
O'er field in red torrents—not languid stream, rill—
Rush deep rivers surging.. Astonishing deeds
High distinguished born heroes strange-mounted on steeds

Jab, Punches, Swing.

That trumpet, roar, bellow. Sometimes, full in van
Where smokes flaming hell, Hill, great chieftain, see! Man
Performed never grander. Glued as if to bull
Of breed Argonian, he spurs, dashes full,
Mad brute loud abellow, distended high tail,
To pierce armored Fat Knight. Bull, Hill, rush asail
Almost into death there, for Olney Hill meets!
But Hill slashing through, Dick swift, headlong unseats
From giraffe, Dick's dapple, gift African king
Submissively proffered with surcingle, ring.
Next David, intrepid, with one savage blow,
Abe Slupsky from lion smites cruelly low,
Carnivorous monster, though called kingly beast,
Upon haunches squatting, cool making damned feast
Fat out luckless Abram. Ah, how learning grieved!
She never, for ages, hadst been so bereaved.
Pod Dismuke, so valiant, through spear-fashioned holes,
Rushed headlong to hell ten cursing, long Poles,
But fell mangled, gory, almost right away,
Head severed by Croker, prodigious in fray.
Dread Richard, Hill's buckler, then next, like green twig
Split neatly from topknot to stern mighty Snigg,
Each moiety falling, all messed up with blood,
Earth soiling disgusting, with dull, heavy thud,
Dick, Injun-like, scalping. So on Richard fought,
Death dealing widely every motion he wrought;
Yet final wast finished, but basely most slain,
Most arear sneaking up, deep sinking in brain
Long, keen, lethal whittle. So famed Richard fell—
Saint some now aver—some declare fiend in hell.
But quick full avenged, for ten Irishmen fierce,
Herr hating most deadly, his middle man pierce,
Sharp daggers inserting. Herr weltered in beer
Out gushing in torrents as foamy, as clear,
As nectar from keg. But Herr, himself, slew
Mad Irish attacking through stench from paunch brew.
Herr's guts spread amain; dug he also clenched hands,
As likewise teeth gnashing, fierce there into sands
Whilst rushed raging soul, dreadful cursing, below,
In death brave, defiant, as in field fronting foe.
But see! Island queen, Amazonian hope,
Reels like her few warriors, unfit more to cope.
Her brave dusky host, with clouts, girdles, torn.
All heaped up, all mangled—dead, pregnant, still-born—
In horrid confusion, whilst thick strewing ground
Love tokens, hearts' volumes, defiled now, abound.
Weep sore, Oh, Hawaii! 'Neath palm tree, on reef,
Lament, Oh, ye lovers! Poor homes waste in grief!
For afar, through ambition, your sweethearts, brown maids,
Tho' matchless in valor, sleep endless. Ne'er shades
Like pure benedictions in even shalt steal,
Nor come sweet as childhood's repentant appeal,
Maids' graves to guard, hallow, but storms, ocean's roar
Trench nameless in sand made, their fate evermore;
Unless—thought abhorrent!—coarse ghouls nightly to
In bags carting bodies to town as rich spoil.

Dick.

Full forty score bodies, all recklessly spread,
Mute testify sadly how maidens fought, bled,
How died, homes forsaking. For what, ask, in end?
For cause most unselfish—unpaid favor friend.
There, too, sturdy Mudsocks in heaps dotting plain;
None braver, more worthy, in war honored slain.
Each wounded in front is. Ne'er Sock yet so base
Displaying to foeman part hinder, but face,
His head high erected, though foe tiger, Sioux,
Rhinoceros, lions, great snakes, naval crew.
There bulwark from Utah—deep-chested, stout-legged,
Now flies, swarming, feast on. No mercy e'er begged;
Craved none craven quarter, but like famed Dacian breed
Waltzed, Gilder songs chanting, to execute, bleed,
To do, to dare—die! Give them, if not tear,
Poor meed, men, of valor—loud, true, feeling cheer.
Well-thewed, bald Adlai, arms, heart, valor-nerved,
Commanding Æolians, he held well reserved
To reinforce quickly if e'er coward flight,
Hard fate, worse defeat, e'er threatened Fat Knight,
Foes noting approaching near valorous chief,
Thundered, "Fly forward!" Like lightning relief
Much needed afforded, hurling fell Hessian horde,
Club, ax, spear, employing—Wash Hesing with sword—
Hill's hirelings hewing, but Adlai cost sore,
For he leading fell, pierced clear through his life's core
An ax "Armour" branded, his own band had dropped.
Sheer through curving ribs crashed blade ere it stopped,
Through firm back protruding, proof potent, skilled hand,
Enforced much with cunning, aimed, engineered brand.
Ad quivered from giraffe, crying out "Holy God!"
Heels upward, head under, striking bloody-soaked sod,
Soil deeply indenting. No warrior e'er gave
That day, e'er before, to heaven more brave,
Upright, worthy spirit. All earth is black night,
But heaven, ye nations, is better, more bright!
So war raged, so fortune, till now trusted few,
Each lot chief surrounding, hack, imprecate, hew,
Howl, loud bawling ribald. But very soon sight
Notes nothing but havoc, dead, Hill, peerless Knight.
There on sick'ning plain, where gay hosts lately shown,
Stand motionless, valiant, warchiefs grand alone,
Fell, grim face to face, earth all reeking with gore,
In hate hellish glaring, fierce bloodhounds of war
Defiance hot snorting. Colossal Knight stood;
Not Juno, Apollo, Mars, combined, 'd look so good.
Knight's neck, clothed with thunder; his puissant, fine thigh;
His chin, speaking valor; his large, flashing eye,
Like buffalo's raging, or fierce forest king's,
When passion possesses—for prey swiftly springs—
Suggesting famed heroes—those immortalized gods
In fact, highest fiction. Knight's foe by all odds
Stood much inferior, yet bulk, training, height,
Declared him fit almost to cope with Fat Knight.
All o'er plain ensanguined, far's Krupp shot could reach,
Piled up, see dead mangled; gory corses block beach;

In blood some are swimming; from some guts protrude;
Many skulls are in fragments, hair matted, all glued,
Brains, gore, congealing; men prone with pale face,
Eyes horridly staring, peering ghastly in space;
Flesh fouling red battlements; heads, stomachs, hearts,
Lights, livers, diaphragms, trunks, thighs, all our parts,
Mixed, awful offal, with flags, banners, faint life
Slow ebbing some places, attest wrath of strife.
On such aceldama, where sicken such scenes,
Rank odors exhaling, war bird raucid screams
Above havoc's harvest, supremest, fell foes,
Each burning volcanic, hellish hating, through nose
Breathing stentorious, each measure, stern eye:
Fate tranquil observing; gods Dagon, Mars, nigh.
Fat Knight's armor's tarnished; all wounds he—in pain—
Scars nobly accepted whilst high piling slain;
All gory, too, foeman, one hideous wound.
In valor each equal, alike each aground,
Beasts under them dying as riders oft charged
Impetuous, grandly. Smaller Hill seemed enlarged
With hate consuming, hairy breast heaving high,
Lips, bloodless, compressed; blood-red flaming eye.
Each helmet-crowned; brass, steel, silver, gold, rest
In form-fitting habit on thigh, bicep, breast,
Each battleax grasping, in scabbard short sword;
On athletic arm shield blows bellic to ward.
Sea, hill, observing, scarce deign to draw breath,
So eager, intently, mark pair planning death.
Knight opens encounter. Hard eye freezing foe,
Fat, leaning forward, attempts coup-de-grace blow,
Hill's head-piece objective. Dave. parrying, quick
Knight's swing duplicating, holding ax as Celt pick,
Both hands grasping handle, whirls circular round,
To give blow momentum, with hiss, whizzing sound,
Huge, death-laden weapon. Fat Knight nimble wheeled,
One step retreating, catching blow on bossed shield,
Sounds giving sonorous. Then freighted thin air,
From hilltop, blue ocean, brave men, ladies fair,
Applause bringing raindrops. But now leaders dance;
They caper, they batter, they imprecate, prance,
Blows falling like snowflakes, or big drops of rain,
Sweat rolling abundant from warriors to plain,
Sweat red, mixed with blood. For nine, ten, minutes thus
Hot heroes slash, sally, contend, caper, cuss.
But strength now is failing. Each foe, lethal bent,
Shows palpable, occular, vigor much spent,
But Hill sure more distressed. Each watching eye sees
Him falter, him languish—his gasping—weak knees.
Fat Knight all see smiling as, taunting, doth sing
War songs exultant. He makes, too, mighty spring,
Hill smiting full, fairly, both feet in grimmed face,
Hill falling flat backward in danger, disgrace.
But short David's anguish, shame mental, deep woe,
For Knight Hill beheaded with one slashing blow,
Then quick grasping trophy, all gore, holding ear,
Head held high aloft. Murder hosts roaring cheer,

Grand, Gory Finale.

Shouts thunderous sounding all o'er bloody plain,
O'er hill, dales adjacent, o'er craft-dotted main.
Then head dashing down, Knight, searching scorned dead,
Quick found Magic Scup, for which prize, fighting, bled,
Died, there valiant thousands. Alive, active fish
In small, gold tank disported to cap crowning wish
Fat Knight long had cherished. But lo, strife at end,
Fat Knight, behold, slowly, doth splendid ascend!
Not like blessed Savior, but upward toward moon,
Reporters to 'scape from perhaps, in balloon,
Which from fleecy clouds, striving hosts' killing o'er,
Had fallen to terra, whence Knight mounted car.
Strong aeronaut outfit, so ascending on high,
Departing alarmed all—brine filling each eye—
Reforming Knight losing. True 'twas bitter fate
Thus sorely, forever, to see nations, lands, state,
Robbed, plundered, ravished. Lamentings, groans, cries,
Some e'en loud cursing God, host venting arise,
Assailing blue concave. But Knight, viewing space,
He calm, cool, collected, so seraphic in face,
Tho' earth's loss regretting, felt infinite gain
Would accrue, him assisting in heaven to reign.
Knight riding, deep reading, manifesto in hand,
He rapidly rising, approached Promised Land,
When heard great commotion. He found, in alarm,
Balloon, now in darkness, in storm, threatened harm—
Aye, likely, destruction! Balloon, smitten sore,
In hail, lightning, zigzag, wind, comets' tails, roar,
Flew—shot upward hellbent. Next door to vast star,
Crash into asteriod dashed fragile car;
Disabled, dismantled, now bottom atop,
Balloon, strange to say, inclined never to drop,
But flew like slim arrow, Fat Knight, tho' obese,
Great manifest reading on apex at ease,
Recalling sad day, many years, years before,
When, astride sorrel charger, he'd ridden so sore.
But, tempest subsiding, sky clearing, in sight,
Behold, heaven's portals ablaze, diamond-bright!
Fat Knight, entrance nearing, called out loudly, clear;
St. Peter, keys bearing, said, "Many a year, [nod,
Knight, you've been expected." Then glad Peter, with
Knight ushered quite proudly before throne of God,
All heaven joy shouting in long, deep acclaim.
God placed Knight beside Him to equally reign.
All heaven fell prostrate; for awhile all adored
In fond, equal worship their old, their new, Lord;
Then harmony vocal in grandeur displays,
Ecstatic'ly sweet, highest climax of praise,
From choir so vast 'twould filled widest zones,
Or torrid on earth. After ravishing tones,
Came Knight's coronation, refreshments, repast,
Post-prandial speaking. Fat Knight spoke at last,
Him God introducing, whereat loudest shout
Went up to gemmed zenith, filled all round about.
Then, plaudits subsiding, Fat Knight went "A-hem!"
Then this address noble made solemn to them:

Colossal Triumph.

"Great Chairman, Good Neighbors: I thank you sincere
For this kind reception, fine music, good-cheer.
It gives me great pleasure to sit at this board;
To meet my old friend here, the—the— (a voice)—'Why,
the Lord!'
It gives me delight, I repeat, to arrive;
To behold how you prosper; see how you all thrive.
I confess some surprise, too. While down below,
While still in New Jersey a long time ago,
I read of these realms, but what I behold—
These walls alabaster, these streets solid gold!
Your air, life and light! These mountains all bloom!
Your marvelous zenith! This rarest perfume!
These angels; these seraphs! This glory! This blaze!
This splendor! This order! These diadems' rays!
Almost confound reason! But yet, in it all,
I think I can fathom true cause of sad Fall.
Your city is splendid. Your country superb,
Surpassing all dreams man, or earth, ever heard.
Your grandeur's appalling. Why, restaurants here
More splendid than palaces below doth appear!
Your music that surges, as oceans that roll,
Holds spell-bound all senses—full intoxicates soul!
Your viands, this vintage, astound and amaze!
Were the latter on earth they'd be drunk all their days!
But, yet, I repeat, I think I can tell
Why Lucifer treasoned and why he proud fell.
Your currency's sound and your foreign affairs
Are excellent all; so's internal repairs;
Your navy is perfect; land forces the same;
In all these departments naught amiss could I name.
But here's your defect, which caused all the storm—
Say, good God Almighty, where's Tariff Reform?"

www.ingramcontent.com/pod-product-compliance
Lightning Source LLC
Chambersburg PA
CBHW020113170426
43199CB00009B/520
* 9 7 8 3 7 4 3 3 4 4 5 5 6 *